MW00380833

PRAISE FOR *NO GOING BACK*

"Governor Kristi Noem is a tremendous leader, one of the best. This book, it's a winner. It exposes the problems we're facing and lays out a fantastic plan to make America great again. You've got to read it!"

— DONALD J. TRUMP, 45TH PRESIDENT OF THE UNITED STATES

"During COVID, Kristi Noem proved she was the governor with the best instincts. This book is grounded in that same common sense and fearless fight for freedom. It's the reminder we need in these dark days to never lose hope in America. Get ready to be inspired!"

— RACHEL CAMPOS-DUFFY, MOM OF NINE AND CO-HOST OF *FOX & FRIENDS WEEKEND*

"In addition to fascinating insights on the inner workings of government, this book will make you bolder! Exactly what America needs."

— CHAYA RAICHIK, CREATOR @LibsOfTikTok

PRAISE FOR *NO GOING BACK*

"An eye-opening message that will surprise and energize patriotic Americans. Those who've been paying attention know she's the real deal. All elected officials need to pay attention to every word from this forward-thinking leader."

— JAMES GOLDEN (AKA BO SNERDLEY), RADIO HOST, PODCASTER, BESTSELLING AUTHOR, AND FORMER RIGHT-HAND MAN TO RUSH LIMBAUGH

"Kristi Noem isn't afraid to challenge the status quo, and neither should we be. This book is the perfect blueprint for young Americans on how to move our nation forward and restore greatness in our country. The time is now."

— RILEY GAINES, ATHLETE, ADVOCATE, WOMAN

NO
GOING
BACK

NO GOING BACK

THE TRUTH ON WHAT'S WRONG WITH POLITICS AND HOW WE MOVE AMERICA FORWARD

KRISTI NOEM

CENTER
STREET®

NASHVILLE   NEW YORK

Center Street
Hachette Book Group
1290 Avenue of the Americas, New York, NY 10104
centerstreet.com
x.com/centerstreet

First Edition: May 2024

Center Street is a division of Hachette Book Group, Inc. The Center Street name and logo are registered trademarks of Hachette Book Group, Inc.

The publisher is not responsible for websites (or their content) that are not owned by the publisher.

The Hachette Speakers Bureau provides a wide range of authors for speaking events. To find out more, go to hachettespeakersbureau.com or email HachetteSpeakers@hbgusa.com.

Center Street books may be purchased in bulk for business, educational, or promotional use. For information, please contact your local bookseller or the Hachette Book Group Special Markets Department at special.markets@hbgusa.com.

Scripture quotations marked (NIV) are from the Holy Bible, New International Version®, NIV®. Copyright © 1973, 1978, 1984, 2011 by Biblica, Inc.™ Used by permission of Zondervan. All rights reserved worldwide. www.zondervan.com. The "NIV" and "New International Version" are trademarks registered in the United States Patent and Trademark Office by Biblica, Inc.™

Scripture quotations marked (ESV) are from The ESV® Bible (The Holy Bible, English Standard Version®), © 2001 by Crossway, a publishing ministry of Good News Publishers. Used by permission. All rights reserved.

Library of Congress Control Number: 2024932629

ISBNs: 9781546008163 (hardcover), 9781546008187 (ebook)

Printed in the United States of America

LSC-C

Printing 1, 2024

This book is dedicated to the people of South Dakota. And not just the ones who voted for me—to all of them. We are a proud people who live off the land and have firm beliefs about right and wrong. Excuses are not accepted here, and a person's handshake and word still mean something. I am a product of this environment. You have helped raise me, taught me, inspired me—and you have given me every opportunity to succeed or fail, based on how hard I worked and my attitude.

I believe every challenge and every success formed who I am today. I am not perfect, but strive to be. I'm complicated, yet look for simple solutions based on common sense. And I am grateful. I am South Dakota, and I love you all. You are great Americans.

CONTENTS

NO GOING BACK

HELP IS NOT ON THE WAY

I did not leave with optimism, I left with the cold reality that help is not on the way in the immediate future.

—NYC MAYOR ERIC ADAMS, DECEMBER 2023, AFTER REQUESTING HELP FROM WASHINGTON, DC, ON THE MIGRANT CRISIS[1]

This is up to us. Nobody's coming here for us. [. . .] If we don't get up and fight for our city, nobody's coming for us.

—ANGRY NYC RESIDENT, SEPTEMBER 2023, INTERVIEWED ABOUT THE MIGRANT CRISIS[2]

I looked at my team and saw fear in their eyes. We could hear explosions and screams in the distance. On the other side of the fence, sounds of shouting and chaos. I smelled what we guessed was tear gas.

We were trapped.

I was responsible for these individuals—my staff and detail team—and we'd never been in this situation before.

Should we stay put or try to make an escape? What vehicle could we use—and does it have lights, sirens, and ammunition? Which route could we take?

This wasn't a trip to some war-torn country. We were standing on the South Lawn of the White House in early August 2020, along with more than a thousand other guests there to hear President Trump's acceptance speech after winning the Republican nomination.

A massive and, at times, violent protest erupted just outside the White House grounds and extended to the National Mall, with chants of "Black Lives Matter!" and "No justice, no peace!"

As the shouting grew louder and other attendees at the president's speech made their way to the exits with the assistance of Secret Service and military officers, my team decided to hold steady. We waited until most of the guests were escorted outside the grounds, then selected an underutilized gate to leave and took the longer way out.

The moment we left the White House grounds we were on our own. If our vehicle was stopped for any reason, we'd be trapped. The streets were filled with rioters, agitators, and those hell-bent on destroying America.[3]

Our vehicle was vulnerable, with no emergency lights or sirens. We drove down several streets only to find them blocked by mobs wielding weapons. Protesters pounded on our vehicle and shouted threats while we passed. My security detail knew to keep going at all costs, even driving on the sidewalk when necessary. Stopping meant danger, and no one would be able to help us.

This can't be real. This can't be America.

After finally reaching safety via underground access to our hotel, with assistance from private security guards, I went to my hotel room, sat down on the bed, and dropped my head into my hands. I was trembling—not from fear but from anger.

I stood up and walked to the hotel window to observe the chaotic streets. This Bible verse from the book of Daniel came to mind: "Praise be to the name of God for ever and ever; wisdom and power are his. He changes times and seasons; he deposes kings and raises up others. He gives wisdom to the wise and knowledge to the discerning. He reveals deep and hidden things; he knows what lies in darkness, and light dwells with him" (Daniel 2: 20–22 NIV).

We were in a dark time in our nation, but I found reassurance in those words. I decided that night to live a life of significance—no matter where that commitment took me —because I believe America is better than the story that night told.

There was no turning back.

Going *back* means more political deception, division, and dysfunction—where insiders benefit and we lose our voice, our freedoms, our way of life, and our future.

To *really* unite and move forward, we need truth from our leaders. In these pages I'll share everything I know about making positive change. We have a historic opportunity, and the stakes couldn't be higher.

Even though I've served in Washington, DC, for eight years and know what a swamp smells like, I am hopeful. I've seen what is possible when we stand together.

We also must face the cold reality that help is not on the way from big government and the establishment. But you already knew that, didn't you? What our country looks like in the next year, and the next decade, is up to us. If we don't step up and fight for our community, for our states, and for our nation, we'll keep sliding backward.

And the entire world will follow our lead, in whichever direction we go.

Trust me, it's not too late, and your voice matters. In my heart I still believe that help is on the way, but not from where most people look.

ONE

WHO'S IN CONTROL?

When you see those messages, remember that
unless you hear it from us, it is not the truth.
—NEW ZEALAND PRIME MINISTER JACINDA ARDERN, MARCH 2020[1]

Under God the people rule.
—OFFICIAL STATE MOTTO OF SOUTH DAKOTA

J ust in case anyone's still feeling nostalgic about the good
old days of "bipartisan cooperation" and normalcy in
Washington, DC—let me offer this gentle encouragement: *Get over it.*

It's true, we don't know if we'll have the same Speaker of
the House in a few months or a few years. I'm okay with that.
Yes, the Republican Party is in disarray. Great! Do you really
think party leaders did a good job when everything was
"normal"?

The mask has been lifted on dysfunction, corruption, and
lies. The propaganda of some members of the media is on full
display. We have new paradigms about what's possible when it
comes to positive change. A multibillionaire business leader,

who never held elected office, became president of the United States and fought for the little guy. A reluctant rancher became a member of Congress, and then a governor. Most important, concerned moms and dads are speaking up at school board meetings and town halls—and seeing results.

Donald Trump and a handful of brave folks broke politics. But what do we do now? Instead of "fixing" politics by going back to the "good old days," let's step into the chaos and move the nation forward. Our best days truly are ahead.

During my time as governor, our team created a leadership development program for state employees, in partnership with a local university, because we want wise leadership at every level of our government. In one of the first classes, I had the honor of answering this question.

"How do you make the really tough decisions?"

Most of the people in the room, and online, were probably five or six layers of bureaucracy away from me. I imagined them on a normal day, in their office, on the other side of the state, wondering, *Why the heck did she do that?* And I knew my fellow South Dakotans sometimes had the same questions about what went into my decisions.

The hard decisions are really not that hard. Here's what I told the class.

A FOUNDATION TO BUILD ON

I was raised in a ranching family, and there was never a difference between girls' chores and boys' chores. Everybody had to work hard, and we were never treated differently. We were a team. While serving in the state legislature and elected to a leadership position, I never thought anything about being a woman in these roles because of the way I had grown up—driving trucks to the grain elevator, chasing cows, or buying and selling livestock and equipment.

But when I ran for governor, a strange thing happened. The fact that I was female suddenly became a big deal to people. Some major Republican donors and a lot of older men told me I didn't have the right anatomy to be governor: *It's a man's job.* They were okay sending a woman to Congress to vote on bills, but to be the CEO of the state was a different matter.

Winning that race for governor was historically significant, and soon I was reminded that the swearing-in ceremony would celebrate the one hundredth anniversary of women obtaining the right to vote in South Dakota, along with the election of the first woman governor of the state. At the event, looking around the rotunda of the crowded capitol building, I noticed so many young girls cheering the moment. They were excited to see someone who looked like them doing something they had never witnessed before in their home state. A woman could be governor!

And then it hit me . . .

Whoa. I better not screw this up. I can't let these girls down. I physically felt a heavy weight hit me as I realized the history we were making. And for the first time I questioned if I was prepared.

As part of the ceremony, there came a time where I had to step forward and take two oaths: to uphold the Constitution of the state of South Dakota, and to uphold the Constitution of the United States. As I laid my hand on my dad's Bible and recited those oaths, literal promises to the people of South Dakota, the role of governor became reassuringly clear.

Two oaths. Well, that's pretty simple, actually. I can do that.

As I lifted my hand from the Bible, the way forward made sense. Early on, I met with our attorneys and asked them to prioritize our state and federal Constitutions, helping us apply them to every decision. First and foremost, I was governor—but what did the Constitution say I should be doing—and not doing?

We apply this same thinking today when it comes to legislation, and the first question is always, is this bill constitutional? Then we ask, what are the long-term impacts of this bill if it is signed into law? What happens if it isn't signed into law? How might this law affect the next generation? (If I sign a bill, we don't only look at immediate implications; we do our best to look at the potential consequences in ten or twenty years.)

Our entire staff goes through a detailed analysis like this for every single bill that's proposed. In effect, we let our Constitution answer the big questions, and then apply my values and what I've promised the people of South Dakota.

Tough decisions and unexpected challenges become easier when we look at them from a solid foundation.

LAND DOESN'T LIE

In 2013, when I was a member of Congress, a huge storm hit western South Dakota that killed tens of thousands of cattle and devastated roads, infrastructure, businesses, and people's homes. Traveling around the state, I sat in kitchens with ranchers in their seventies and eighties who were sobbing because they'd lost their entire cattle herd—which meant they not only lost that year's calf crop, but they also lost the "manufacturing plant"—the mother cows. They felt like personal failures because they were proud of how they cared for their livestock and were good stewards of these animals that depended on them. Their ability to pay their bills and make land payments was gone overnight. They saw little hope of passing their way of life on to their children and grandchildren.

All a farmer or rancher has to give to their children is the land. They don't have a pension fund or a retirement account, but they are stewards of one of the most precious natural resources. The land cannot lie. It reflects the care that's put into it. Stewardship choices might not become apparent for five or ten years. For my husband, Bryon, and me, the ranch will tell our story to our kids, grandkids, great-grandkids, and beyond.

While our families have farmed and ranched in South Dakota for generations, the ranch we live on was purchased by my dad when I was a young girl. When he first showed it to me I was struck by how different it was from the farm we lived on. It was rugged land—unbroken but full of potential. I told him I wanted to live there someday, and he replied, "Someday you can buy it from me." No free lunch in my dad's world.

You can't be a farmer or rancher and not be a long-term thinker. And I happen to believe elected officials should always make decisions with future generations in mind. It's the same way you and I must take care of our land, these United States of America.

My dad died unexpectedly in an accident on our farm when I was twenty-two years old, married, and pregnant with our first child. The loss was devastating. He was our rock. The fact that we ran a family business together didn't make it any easier to look forward. Quite the opposite. The crops and the animals still needed the same care as they did the day before, and everywhere we looked there were reminders of him. But we couldn't just stop or even take time to grieve. It was a hard season for all of us.

As the months passed, I assumed the responsibility of being general manager of the ranch. I had learned over the years about how government policies impacted our livelihood, but overseeing all the operations was eye-opening. The government had its hand in everything we did.

I never imagined a life in politics and never dreamed about having a career in Washington. My role models were not Nancy Pelosi or Paul Ryan. I was blessed with better examples—my parents, my siblings, and my neighbors. Truth be told, I had a fondness for John Wayne too. Even though I didn't want to be involved in politics, politics kept getting involved with our business. Very involved.

In fact, the very survival of the ranch was threatened by the "death tax," which was a provision in the federal tax code that creates double taxation—when earned and upon death. It's the most unfair and destructive tax in America.

Additionally, important agriculture policy decisions at the state and federal level were seemingly made with no input from us and our peers. I started attending local meetings to understand what was happening and why. It wasn't for political reasons; our family was never really partisan. In fact, as a result of speaking up and asking questions at those gatherings, former US senator Tom Daschle encouraged me to run for public office—as a Democrat!

I took half his advice, ran for a state legislative seat as a Republican, and won.

During my four years in that role, I was often asked to consider running for Congress. I got really good at saying *no thanks*. But in 2010, something changed in me, and the requests to run for Congress started to come from across the nation, which I detail in my first book. My decision—and transition—was profound and painful for my whole family. Even though it was never my life's goal to serve in Washington, after much consideration and many family discussions, we made the decision to take on an incumbent Democrat member of Congress for South Dakota's lone seat in the US House of Representatives.

The race was one of the most closely watched campaigns in the country, and part of a national wave in opposition to President Obama's and Nancy Pelosi's leadership. As a result of enormous amounts of hard work with our team, we won. That's when things really started to get interesting. It was the end of 2010, but the beginning of an adventure we never imagined.

As I have done with everything in my life, being a wife, mom, businesswoman, rancher, and public office holder, I was determined to give this new role everything I had.

INTO THE FRAY

The word "compliant" has never been used to describe my personality, and I'll admit the leap to Washington, DC, was daunting. I was hungry for wisdom and raised to believe we can learn something valuable from every person we meet. That approach was immediately tested in Congress, and I concluded that sometimes we learn from others is what *not* to do.

I expected to be working with normal Americans—but so many of the people I met had no idea what normal America was like. The place was broken, but the culture was well established.

When I first ran for Congress, I hired the consultants recommended by our senior US senator, John Thune. And I listened to them. The experts told me to cut my hair. No more big earrings. Definitely no cowgirl boots at certain functions. They recommended basic training on how to walk properly in high heels. (Yes, really.) Before one event, one of the senator's biggest supporters quietly handed me a bottle of fingernail polish remover and told me to never wear that color again—only natural was acceptable.

They're the experts, I guess, and they know how to get things done here. So, I started dressing like a ninety-year-old woman with shortish hair and boring nails—not that there's anything wrong with that, but it wasn't authentic for me.

Does all this sound a bit weird and shallow? Are you surprised that the first order of business from political experts was focused on hair, makeup, and wardrobe? Just wait . . . there's more.

Somehow, I managed to run a business and win a seat in the state legislature by being myself and speaking my mind. But when I ran for Congress, all of a sudden I was thrown into an alternate universe where conformity was valued over results. *This is how things are done if you want to work in Washington.*

As a newly elected representative with a young family, I was eager for guidance about navigating all the decisions, committees, and schedules. Senator Thune was very helpful in many areas, but he also suggested I consider *not* seeking an appointment on the House Committee on Agriculture. He went on to explain that it was quite likely that no farm bill would pass that year, and it could be political baggage to serve on the committee that didn't do the hard work to get

WHO'S IN CONTROL?   13

this important policy for South Dakota across the finish line. The rationale was that it would be smarter to stay off the committee and not take ownership of the delay of the bill. I was surprised but took his advice, requested other committee assignments, and sought a spot on the leadership team advising the Speaker of the House on national conservative policy.

My whole life until that point focused on agriculture; I knew it inside and out. Looking back, I remember being a bit embarrassed at how quickly I lost my footing in the new environment and relied on advice more than my own instincts and experience.

I was elected by my colleagues as co-president of the freshman class, which gave me a seat at the leadership table. I joined the Education and Workforce, Armed Services, and Natural Resources committees—and South Dakota's collective heads exploded. It was the first time in history that their representative wasn't on the Agriculture Committee, and everyone wondered why. Loudly.

Prior to Congress, I served for years on the committee that oversaw all the farm programs in the state of South Dakota, and now I'd chosen to not be on the committee that impacted our number one industry and ensured conservation programs were in place to preserve our land. Every weekend when I went home to have meetings and talk with people, instead of reporting on all the good work that was happening, I answered endless questions about why I didn't care about agriculture.

Within weeks, I asked the Speaker of the House, John Boehner, to put me on the Agriculture Committee, in addition to my other committees and nine subcommittees. It was a heavy workload and more of a time commitment than most members of Congress had at the time.

Members of the old guard, who want to hold on to their power for as long as possible, go out of their way to convince newly elected representatives that they can't possibly navigate government without their guidance. This is the very same lie they tell the American people: "You don't know how complicated Washington is. Just vote for us, and we'll handle it." In its purest form, that's what a constitutional republic is. But the reality has become corrupted almost beyond recognition.

It doesn't hurt to take advice and ask questions, but in the end a leader must follow their instincts and do what's right for those they serve.

CONTROLLING THE NARRATIVE

One glaring example of what's wrong with politics was my first committee hearing in DC. I was a little nervous but very prepared with questions for the invited witnesses. As I entered the meeting, one of the chairman's staff members handed me a list and said, "Here are the questions you're going to ask."

"Oh, thanks. But I have my own questions ready," I answered as I waved away their paper.

"No, you don't understand," they responded with that same fake grin I'd been seeing around town. "You will ask *the chairman's* questions." And they shoved the paper back in front of my face.

"No, I will not. I've studied the issues. I have good questions, and I want to ask them."

The smile vanished. "Listen, this is how it's done, Congresswoman Noem. The chairman wants a certain narrative to come out of this committee, and this list of questions are part of it."

I took the sheet of paper from his hands and said thank you. And when it became my turn to ask questions, I used my own. No one was going to tell me how to spend my time. And, in my humble opinion, my questions and comments were better than their script.

I never imagined members of Congress showing up in committees without doing their own homework and without bringing up perspectives that mattered to their constituents. Most were just playing their part in the theater. Sometimes their office staff worked with the committee staff to add a local reference, but it always fit the agenda the chairman wanted to pursue. That's not how we worked in the state legislature in South Dakota, and it wasn't going to work for me.

There's a particular definition of anger that resonates with me. Anger comes from a recognition that something is wrong, and it needs to be made right, and for me it turned into determined resolve to fight for the people of my state. From that day in committee forward, this helped me be effective. It does no good to get angry on behalf of myself. But when you channel that anger and determination on behalf of others, you can outthink the bastards. Outsmart them. Be better and do better.

The haters, in both parties, were watching, and waiting for the "farm girl" to be a dummy. Sure, I made mistakes, and I still do, but I was not about to abandon my values and what I knew to be true. And this resolve would be tested, again and again.

Those haters are still there. But they no longer think I'm a dummy. Now they are scared because they know I'm a fighter, I'm smart, and I'm usually right because I do my own homework.

CONGRESSIONAL VOTER FRAUD

Here's another interesting tidbit about life in DC. Members of Congress often vote two or three times a day, on multiple bills and resolutions. When most members walk out of their office on the way to the House floor to cast their votes, they are handed cards from their staff.

Vote #1: No.

Vote #2: Yes.

Vote #3: Motion to recommit. No.

You get the idea. I received these helpful notes as well. There's no problem with simple reminders to avoid confusion, but there's a big problem when members of Congress skip the research and simply take orders from their party's leaders or staffers. And this happens on both sides of the aisle. I wish I had a nickel for every time I heard a member of Congress say on the House floor, "Hey is this vote eight or nine? Because my staff says I should be a yes on eight but a no on nine. Which is it?"

Here's my assessment after eight years working on Capitol Hill: the majority of my peers often had no idea what they were voting on or what was in the bill's text. Does that surprise you? Disgust you? It sure did me. I'm sorry to say, that's how things have been done for a long time. It's a backward way to run the country.

COMMAND AND CONTROL AND COVID

In 2020, dysfunction mutated into dictatorship. The COVID-19 pandemic changed our country and changed me. It almost killed us, and I'm not talking about a virus. Most of the American population was at high risk for being controlled. Tens of millions were infected. Folks in Washington, DC, and state capitals were the super-spreaders.

"Listen to us. We're the experts. Follow our science. Do not do your own research, and by no means draw your own conclusions."

When the virus started to spread across the world, the public health experts told me our state would have ten thousand South Dakota residents in the hospital on a single day. (The most we ever had was six hundred, by the way.) Hospitals would be overwhelmed, and massive triage centers needed to be constructed in just a few weeks. A prognosis like that will test your convictions and scare the hell out of you.

My staff and I watched the news as, one by one, states announced unthinkable lockdowns with unimaginable fear-mongering and threats. Spoiler alert, in case you missed it: South Dakota was the only state that stayed open. More on this topic later, because these same scenarios will undoubtedly play out again in the future, and we need to be prepared.

Whether it's a virus, threats of terrorism, or economic upheaval, the response of the establishment is always the same: Make more rules. Consolidate power in Washington. It's about control. And that's what so many Democrats—and Republicans—cling to. You know what they say: "Never let a crisis go to waste."

WHO'S REALLY IN CONTROL?

Any elected official can talk about how broken our government is, but their proposed solutions always seem to involve more money, new programs—and *(shocker!)* reelection to another term.

I still don't want to be in politics. Politics actually sucks. Seriously, the mob does not care who they destroy to get the power they want. But *serving* is energizing and rewarding. I share this to encourage you, because you don't have to *want* to be in politics to be a part of the future—and move your community, state, and country forward.

It's possible to follow your interests and live a life of significance, knowing that what you are doing every day is helping people and protecting freedom. We need people who are willing to stop being selfish by only thinking of their own comfort and find reward in sacrificing to save the greatest experiment in human history, the United States of America.

In South Dakota our motto is "Under God the people rule." Every day we're doing our best to make this a reality. We know what backward looks like—look at California or New York. And we know what forward looks like, because we've seen progress in South Dakota and other conservative-led states.

Right now, to a large extent, the establishment—elected and unelected bureaucrats—are in control. Their hold is starting to slip, but the establishment will only lose control when people like you decide to take control. It's a decision that requires action, though. And I'm going to give you a blueprint.

In these pages I'm honored to share my mistakes, our successes, the truth about how things are, and how we can move America forward. Once you've seen what's possible, there's no going back. And why would you want to? Our best days are ahead.

STEP FORWARD

No matter how savvy you are, it's so easy to get swept into the "that's just how it's done here" mentality when you enter a new arena. Dysfunctional, self-serving political culture is like a rushing river. As you step in, be ready for how powerful the current is.

We've all seen newly elected officials—ones we believed would fight for our interests—swept downstream into the swamp.

Don't be deceived by the myth that the experts know best about how to get things done. Look around and ask yourself if anything is actually moving forward in the right direction.

Don't believe the lie that government is complex. Honestly, doing the right thing isn't easy, but it is straightforward. Hold tight to your values, base your foundation on the Constitution, and let's step forward.

TWO

CONGRESS, CAMPAIGNS, AND CASH

> What happened to you, Dillon? You
> used to be someone I could trust.
>
> —DUTCH (ARNOLD SCHWARZENEGGER) IN PREDATOR[1]

> *Well, I can always go back to farming,*
> *and that sounds pretty good.*
>
> —KRISTI NOEM, DURING EVERY CONGRESSIONAL
> REELECTION CAMPAIGN

I never understood how someone elected to Congress could develop a case of "constituent amnesia" until I spent a few months in Congress. I met members of Congress who stopped going home, stopped living like normal people—doing their own grocery shopping, driving themselves places, going to ball games, or pumping their own gas. It seemed that once these folks got elected, they started thinking they were really big deals. Their priorities changed because how they spent their time changed and who they talked to changed.

They developed amnesia, almost like they forgot where they came from. I worked hard not to fall into that trap, but honestly it wasn't that hard when I was still a mom to young kids, a wife to a husband who ran a small business, the children's pastor at our church, and a volunteer 4-H leader. I tried to keep my life as normal as possible to keep stability for my family, but it also helped me do my job better—with a clearer perspective.

In 2012, the people who put me in office—and those who voted not to—were getting upset about the lack of progress on the farm bill. The farm bill had always been a bipartisan piece of legislation that Republicans and Democrats supported, recognizing the need for food security in our country.

The farm bill is a piece of legislation that has all federal policies for risk management programs for farmers, including crop insurance, disaster relief programs, the nutrition title (aka food stamps), forestry conservation programs, and programs for low-income women, infants, and children.

These policies were always combined because the farm bill is our food policy. America decided years ago that it was in our best interest to have a safe and affordable food supply that we grow ourselves. That is what the farm bill was meant to ensure for all people, and it has always been bipartisan. But we have seen the legislation become more politicized as food stamps became abused—and as politicians subsidized certain commodities for certain areas of the country to benefit whichever representative had the power to write the bill.

The consequences of politicizing agriculture have allowed foreign countries to buy sections of our food supply chain and larger farms to swallow up smaller ones. It's in our best interest to have many small farmers rather than a handful of huge corporations.

Everyone eats, and everyone needs a farm bill to ensure they can put food on the table. In 2013 the bill went to a vote— and failed. Needlessly. And definitely for political reasons.

A Republican representative had added an amendment to the bill that proposed work requirements for SNAP, or food stamp, recipients. I support more accountability for welfare or assistance programs, but the added baggage caused many of my colleagues on the Democrat side of the aisle to vote against it. And Republicans knew that would happen. They didn't care. Congress was playing partisan games, while farmers waited for a safety net while they grew the world's food supply. Remember the risks farmers take. They are the biggest gamblers I know. They literally go to the bank, borrow millions of dollars, and bury it in the dirt. Then they hope it rains, hope the crops produce, and hope for a good harvest, so they can pay their bills. This is an oversimplification, of course, but it is reality. Farmers need a safety net, and Americans need farmers.

Republican Eric Cantor was House majority leader and a fan of the "poison pill" food stamp work requirement, and I was pissed. He not only supported the amendment to add the policy; he actually went to the House floor and spoke on behalf of the amendment, which is very rare for someone in leadership to do. Cantor seemed to be willing to cause the entire bill to fail in order to get this change in statute. An important piece of legislation died and nobody seemed to care. Days later, at the next GOP conference meeting, Cantor presented the floor agenda, but there was no mention of the farm bill.

When it came time for an open floor discussion, I walked forward to one of the conference microphones and asked firmly, "Mr. Leader, could you please return to the podium, and could you please tell me the plan for passing the farm bill?"

He slowly rose from his seat, returned to the podium at the front of the room, and summarized what happened. He left out the fact that an amendment he supported was the cause of the bill's failure. *Too bad, so sad, we'll give it a try next year*, was my interpretation.

"Leader Cantor, this is unacceptable for you not to have a plan for action on the bill," I said. I then explained how important this bill was for every single member in the room who had constituents who needed to eat. *Did I just say that out loud?* Yep. This bill was our food policy for the nation. I questioned his leadership abilities and told him I expected a plan. I even told him and others in the room that I questioned their concern for our constituents—and unless this was rectified, they shouldn't expect my support for their upcoming bills. I returned to my seat and the meeting was quickly adjourned.

I walked back to my office, opened the door to hurry into a meeting I was late for, and was surprised to see my chief of staff standing there, arms crossed, waiting for me.

"What did you do?" he asked.

He informed me that I just received an "invitation" to Cantor's office. I filled my chief of staff in on the situation on our walk back to the leader's office. When we arrived, we were informed this would be a "members only" meeting. I was ushered into Cantor's private office, and his staffer scurried out the door quickly. Cantor was pacing the floor, and I could tell he wasn't happy. Once the door was closed he started in. "You do *not* do that to me! You don't talk to me like that in front of the whole conference!"

As he went on, I stood my ground. "It's past time for the farm bill to get done," I answered. "I have no intention of letting you or anyone else in Republican leadership off the hook. This needs to be a priority. I'm not going to wait anymore." Long story short, with the help of my colleagues, including Cantor, the bill was signed into law.

It is possible to get things done in Washington, but it takes guts and what some may call stubbornness. And sometimes it takes money.

MONEY

Let's go there. No matter how talented or successful you might be, and it doesn't matter if you're the best politician, public speaker, or smartest policy person in the world—our system requires money. Some say money is the lifeblood of politics. I disagree, but it does have a role in the drama. Without finances, effective communication with the public is almost impossible, and we need all the tools necessary to push back on fake news. You can't win without financial support. Believe me.

In high school I did well in sports, received excellent grades, and won some awards. I earned money for what I needed. Any success I experienced was simply the result of putting in the work and bringing my best. My biggest challenge in running for office was the fact that I couldn't be successful without other people's help. In hindsight, that realization was a good thing.

My fundraising speeches were, and still are, pretty unusual, and go something like this: "This is the worst part of the job—asking for your money and your time. I hate it. But I also know that I cannot win unless you help me. So I will promise you this: I promise that I'll be a good investment. I promise to work hard every day and be exactly who you know me to be. I'll always be accountable and tell you why I voted the way I did."

This seems to resonate with folks, and I'm glad, because it's the absolute truth. Most people assume politicians love raising money. Not me; I'm an introvert. Even today as governor, I raise money, do a lot of interviews, and spend a lot of time posting to social media about what's happening in our state. I don't sit in front of the camera because it feeds my ego. It's misery most of the time, and it still makes me nervous. The same goes for speeches. I'd much rather sit on a stage and answer people's questions rather than stand at a podium and lecture. That's just how I roll.

"IT'S JUST SOUTH DAKOTA"

The first year and a half in Congress, I didn't have a vehicle in Washington, and most of my staff were young or too broke to have one either. We didn't have much money, but we did own a 2001 Buick LeSabre that had belonged to Bryon's grandpa. It was our family car for a while, and then our daughter drove it for a while—demolition derby style. That poor car had smashed fenders and a crushed roof from a rollover accident on an icy winter day, but it ran pretty well and was paid for.

Getting around Washington is not easy. So one day I said to Bryon, "Why don't you take a road trip with one of your buddies and bring me the Buick to drive around DC?"

He agreed, and a few weeks later he arrived in our congressional chariot. Other than the fact that it didn't have air-conditioning (we fixed that later), my staff and I kind of enjoyed driving that old Buick around. It was quite the contrast to all the blacked-out Suburbans zooming through DC. After President Trump was elected, it was still our official limo. When I was invited to meetings at the White House, the Secret Service took notice.

For the first couple visits, as our sketchy-looking, dented car approached the gates, security jumped into high alert to intercept us. No doubt they thought we were people who didn't belong at the White House, and I can't blame them. But after a few visits, they began to recognize us. "It's okay!" they'd shout to each other. "It's just South Dakota!" as they waved us through the gates.

We made our mark at those White House meetings— literally. That old Buick had a bad oil leak, and I'd smile every time we spotted our favorite parking space. I'm sure it's still there.

As out of place as our ride was in DC, that's how I felt about the norms of campaigns and the money that fueled them. You need resources, but those resources should be used to do your job representing your people—not living the high life. Because most Americans don't know where or how campaign money is spent—and most politicians aren't very transparent about it—I hope what I share will help. You deserve to know.

WHERE DOES THE MONEY GO?

Most Americans would guess much of the money goes toward TV ads, and they're right, although those ads also run on a growing number of online and broadcast platforms today. Elections are an industry, employing consultants for every kind of media—all interconnected and in many cases scratching each other's backs. (Candidates come and go, but consultants "rove" around for decades. It's one of the few professions where there seem to be no consequences for losing.)

As with everything related to the political arena, a megadose of skepticism is key. With every campaign I asked more and more questions, because accountability seemed like a rare commodity.

It is possible to work hard to win elections and not lose your soul, and my most recent reelection campaign for governor was by far the most fun. Why? Because our efficiency was the best ever. I personally reviewed every proposal, invoice, and mileage report, and I knew where every dollar went. Instead of approving vague proposals for ad buys, I required specific details. Invoices had to show exactly what was delivered. And we won by a bigger margin than ever before. Having this level of transparency and accountability brings confidence and takes a lot of the yuck out of campaigning.

Most candidates just don't know they can ask those kinds of questions, and many consultants aren't used to being asked. Again, there was a learning curve for me and my team, but my experience managing several businesses definitely helped. There's no reason a campaign can't run like a business—with accountability to its board of directors and investors.

THE GREEN WAVE

Speaking of green, can we talk about 2022 and the "Red Wave" that never made a splash?

Yes, the strength of individual candidates matters. But the fact that our party did not achieve a majority in the US Senate was a failure by the Republican National Committee

(RNC). Ronna McDaniel's leadership was in the spotlight during the 2023 presidential debates and, I must say, rightfully so. Ronna is a friend, and I respect her, but no business executive gets to produce poor results and still keep the top job—unless you work for Disney. When President Trump lost in 2020, the RNC assured us they already had a legal team ready to look into every question of fishy voting. Weeks passed. Months passed. Nothing.

I've spoken with Ronna many times in the past several years and would never write anything here that I haven't said to her directly. In my experience, the RNC doesn't help with messaging, the polling isn't shared with candidates, funds are often directed in mysterious ways, and tangible results are often hard to find.

The pundits were quick to blame former president Trump for the failures of the 2022 election cycle. But we failed again in 2022 because we didn't reach the hearts and minds of the American people. Instead of leading them with a vision to move forward, we *followed.* We got lazy, and no one was held accountable. (I have similar sentiments about the National Republican Congressional Committee, but I am hopeful about 2024 and willing to help.)

Many Republicans thought that since the Biden administration was such a train wreck, we could just talk a big game and coast into victory. Let's learn this lesson for 2024 and beyond: it doesn't matter how bad the other team is; we have to do the work to prove our team is better. And we need to inspire with a hopeful vision. We have to tell people what we are *for.* Just being against something or someone isn't enough.

As much as I detest the campaign game, it's the only game in town. And Republicans need to wise up about how some big Democrat fish (*cough . . . Mark Zuckerberg*) mess with elections. South Dakota is a relatively small state by population. It's much too easy for an outside group to create a huge impact here, as opposed to in the bigger media markets like Florida or Texas. A few million spent in Florida or Texas is a drop in the bucket, but that same amount of money in a "small" state can really move the numbers.

Every state, big and small, sends the same number of senators to Washington. South Dakota and other states like ours are more important than people might think. And trust me, Democrats try to sway elections in our state every chance they get.

WHAT TO DO?

When it comes to supporting candidates for office, there are lots of ways to join in. Your time, your money, your voice, your prayers—a million different things you can do. Consider this when you receive a piece of mail or see an ad from your favorite candidate. If you can, send a donation, however small it may be. Yeah, really. This support actually helps.

Then brace yourself, because you'll receive more mail, emails, and maybe even texts. Last election year my mom called me with a question. *(Sorry, Mom. I gotta tell this story.)*

She said, "Kristi, I'm getting so many text messages from Kevin McCarthy. How is he? Sounds like he needs my help! I donated twenty dollars yesterday, should I send him another twenty today?"

"That's sweet, Mom. But Kevin McCarthy does not need your money. He does a good job raising dollars from all the rich guys. You keep your money." Then I asked her to dig deep and write the biggest possible donation to my campaign. Okay, I'm kidding about that last part.

But the fact is, no donation is "small," because they all matter—to the giver and the receiver. I still advised my mom to keep her money and let Kevin know her heart was in the right place.

A donation is an investment in a candidate, and it's safe to say that if you're spending hard-earned money supporting someone, you will be voting for that person on Election Day. And votes are what counts—literally.

THE BIGGEST CHALLENGE FOR CONGRESS AND STATE LEGISLATORS

Whether it's in the state legislature or Congress, the biggest challenge for any representative is keeping perspective. How do you keep perspective? The primary way is to surround yourself with people who remind you who you are and where you come from. In simpler terms, you need to be with *normal* people.

As President Dwight D. Eisenhower said, "You know, farming looks mighty easy when your plow is a pencil, and you're a thousand miles from the corn field."[2]

On breaks from Congress I'd go home and cashier at a grocery store on a weekend, or sometimes work a shift at the local gas station and listen to people talk. Our kids' sporting events were another wonderful way to stay grounded. These days were always perfect reminders that what people were talking about with friends and neighbors was the opposite of what the Washington crowd was obsessed with.

Believe me, when elected officials get together, they talk a lot about how to get reelected. When I considered the possibility every two years that I might lose my job in Congress, I always thought, *Well, this may one day look good on my résumé, but maybe I'll go back to farming. That would be nice.*

This perspective helped. During the COVID-19 pandemic, as governor, I actually encouraged people to stop watching the national news all day and instead talk to people they trusted in their state and their community. And I said the same thing to other governors. We all make better decisions when we focus on what matters—and focus on *who* matters around us.

TELLING THE TRUTH

Within six months of my first term in Congress, a funding bill passed to keep the government open, and it raised the debt ceiling. Several spending reforms and caps on spending were tied to the debt ceiling so, over the long run, it was going to reduce our national debt and start to turn the tide on government spending. This was a classic example of ugly policy tied to good policy.

Everybody in South Dakota who supported me could not figure out why I would support such a horrific bill. Our national debt was rising. I'd been extremely critical of those in Congress who repeatedly endorsed bigger budgets with no accountability to the taxpayers. I campaigned on being different. When this vote occurred in my first term, people at home wondered if I'd changed so soon.

I came home and immediately scheduled town hall meetings, and I was greeted there by hundreds and hundreds of people who were terribly offended that I voted for the bill. I endured the yelling and did my best to answer the questions honestly. It was hell, but those meetings were the best thing I could have done.

It's quite possible that no one left that meeting with a different view of the vote. But I believe everyone left with more respect for each other. And even if they disagreed with me, I think they understood why I voted the way I did and respected me for talking with them about it. In Congress, it wasn't my job to vote how I was told to vote. My job was to get the facts, seek wisdom, and make the final decision.

But Kristi, doesn't that sound a lot like "Trust me, you don't understand how things work in DC"?

No, there's a big difference. And the difference is transparency, which I abide by to this day. Agree or disagree, but you'll always know where I stand, what I believe is right, and why.

A STUPIDLY SIMPLE SOLUTION?

How can we move Congress forward—or rather, get Congress out of our way?

First, let's face the truth about why our legislative branch has fallen into a swamp. As described in the opening story, politicians start with a good idea for a bill. (Okay, I'm being generous, but stay with me.) But this single-purpose bill is combined with other bills, and amendments are attached, until it turns into some sort of Frankenstein piece of legislation, thanks to the Speaker of the House or party majority leaders.

A farm bill becomes dependent on welfare reform, which hinges on a budget item for the military or includes a few million dollars to fund an art installation featuring the work of left-handed poly-gendered potters. This snowballs until the piece of legislation is so convoluted that *no* representative is happy (and every citizen who dares to pay attention is disgusted). Then they vote. But don't worry, the vote happens so fast that almost no one reads what's in the bill.

Here's an alternative, and it's been proposed many times before. Congress creates and votes on *single-issue* bills. (Can you hear political insiders rolling their eyes right now?) Yes, representatives would put forth an idea for legislation and actually do the work of talking with other members of Congress to win their support.

Instead of coalitions of compromise holding their nose and passing garbage bills, they could talk to each other about important matters—even to those across the aisle.

When I arrived in Congress, I had very negative opinions about some of my Democrat colleagues—until I met with them about issues we all cared about. Healthy debate happened, education happened, and respect was forged.

The establishment hates this idea (which is reason enough to love it), but I'm telling you, one-subject bills would fundamentally improve the way DC operates right now. Imagine the new way the media would cover important votes if there was one issue on the table. Imagine how much easier it would be for us to talk to our representatives about the issues that are most important to us.

And the best part of this idea is that the Speaker of the House could implement it—today!

COUNTING THE COST

It might be hard to believe, but Congress can be a lonely place. That was my experience, anyway.

Almost every week, for days at a time, I was away from my husband, kids, family, and friends. On Sunday nights, our youngest child, Booker, knew I'd be traveling the next day, and that when he woke up Monday morning, I'd already be gone. He knew I would be home at the end of the week, but that seemed like an eternity to a seven-year-old. I dreaded the tearful moments when I tucked him into bed on Sunday nights.

I'd leave my house at four o'clock Monday morning; drive two hours to the airport; park my car; drag my suitcase through a dark, empty parking lot that was often cold, wet, or snowy; and board a six thirty a.m. flight to Minneapolis. After a four-hour layover, I'd board a flight to DC, arriving just in time to go to the floor and vote. At the end of the day, I'd walk back to my office and sleep on the couch. Glamorous, huh?

In Washington there were endless meetings—good and bad, productive and wasteful, hopeful and discouraging. But I spent 80 percent of my days by myself. Even with all those interactions, I felt completely alone, because nobody there really knew me or cared about me. No one there grew up with me or had shared memories. Many times during that first year in Congress I battled the thought, *What have I done, and how can I undo this?*

To many people watching on social media or TV, it might seem like I and other representatives were living the dream—having press conferences, attending important meetings, hanging out with all the political "stars," and traveling around the world. I count many of those activities an honor. But most of all during those years, I was worried about my kids. I missed my family, my horse, and my home.

Was it worth it? Wonderful opportunities have opened up for our family, and we try to focus on those blessings. But there's a heavy price to be paid. Bryon and I have always told our kids that experiences can make you stronger, or you can use them as an excuse. We also remind them, and ourselves, that what we've done is *not* difficult compared to what other people have done for their country. Not even close. You know what's hard? Serving in our military, running a small business, the often thankless job of nursing, being in law enforcement, and taking care of your kids as a stay-at-home mom.

Would I advise you to go into public service? Yes. If you believe you're the best person for the role at that moment, go for it. Doing anything meaningful is hard and requires sacrifice, but it's worth it. Bryon and I talk about this a lot. I'd quit if we believed there was somebody better for the job—and I'd be their biggest ally on the campaign trail.

The same introspection is required on any level of service to our great country. If you speak up at a PTA meeting or run for the school board, your life will change. Conversations at your kids' sporting events will be different. You'll find out who your true friends are, which is always good. Once you step into the arena, there's no going back.

As Teddy Roosevelt encouraged us, "In the long run, success or failure will be conditioned upon the way in which the average man, the average woman, does his or her duty, first in the ordinary, every-day affairs of life, and next in those great occasional cries which call for heroic virtues. [. . . T]he main source of national power and national greatness is found in the average citizenship of the nation."[3]

Thankfully, our kids have stayed true to who they are and where they came from. Here are some reasons I'm so proud of our daughters. More on our son, Booker, later.

KASSIDY AND KYLE, KENNEDY AND TANNER

Kyle and our daughter Kassidy got married the summer after I was elected governor. The ceremony was in Custer State Park, in the Black Hills. Kyle's family are farmers and ranchers from South Dakota, and it was a big, beautiful wedding.

This was our first opportunity melding two families together. Kyle's family probably had to be pretty patient with us, because I can't imagine a more miserable situation for a family than marrying into the governor's family, who had just gone through a very tough election. They gave us a lot of grace.

Kyle is extremely talented and well spoken. He serves on a city council and several boards at the state level to which he was elected. Kyle is also a smart businessman and passionate about hunting. There is nobody more fun to hunt with, because he loves to share his love for the sport and truly enjoys seeing someone else be successful. Kyle will go out of his way to find opportunities for people to get new experiences and have fun. He is a fantastic dad, and one reason is because his kids are going to experience a lot of really cool things in life.

I don't know of a better mother than Kassidy. She was created to be a mother, and she can do ten things at one time and remain perfectly calm. She can be eight months pregnant and carrying a forty-pound baby around in her arms while she's doing her job, cleaning her kitchen, snowed in, and changing the oil in her pickup truck. She's what I would call a renaissance woman. Kassidy is a commonsense person with an amazing ability to solve problems and be very forthright.

Tanner and Kennedy had known each other for five or six years before they married in 2022. They wanted a small wedding, away from the hoopla around me, and I understand. We were in the thick of my reelection campaign for governor.

The wedding was in Sedona, Arizona, which was the ideal setting for a fun, intimate ceremony. Tanner's mom and dad gave a very touching speech at the wedding, recounting stories about their little boy. They've never once heard him say a negative word about anyone, and that's been my experience as well. I imagine someone could mug him and take his wallet, and his response would be "I wonder what happened to them in life to make them do that." He might be the most positive individual I've ever met, and he is a study of leadership.

He's passionate about being successful and mentoring other leaders. I think his proudest moments are when he sees someone on his team doing very well. He celebrates successes in unexpected ways. Instead of a dinner out, he'll take the entire team to a beach for a weekend.

Kennedy was indispensable for many reasons when I was elected governor. At just twenty-two years of age, she was on my transition team, at the request of many people around me. But one way that I and the staff appreciated was her role as a liaison—a translator, really—for me. She served in my office for two years, handling all my federal liaison work and doing policy for three agencies. She is incredibly gifted, and I wish she could see in herself what I see. She is a problem solver with a heart.

STEP FORWARD

When challenges came, I reminded myself that I could always go back to work on the ranch. That was always plan A, and still is. Plan B was serving the people of my state—I truly love the opportunity, and I'm giving it my all. May I suggest that there are too many people whose plan A is politics. They have no plan B, and that's why they're so desperate to win—and why they shouldn't be in public service. They have no other life and no other skills to go home to. That's something to consider when voting.

Are you busy with your everyday life? Do you have a career or skill set? Is there something you're pissed about and want to change in your neighborhood, town, state, or nation? We need people like you to be involved.

Go raise a ruckus. Help set some stuff straight, and then get back home and enjoy your plan A.

To paraphrase what I learned from author Arthur Brooks, great leaders never get angry on behalf of themselves; they get mad on behalf of the weak. Consider my experience with the farm bill. My constituents certainly aren't weak, but they don't have the power to pass legislation. Tenacity and standing up for what's right made the difference.

Congress and campaigns can be ugly monsters. And yes, money is part of the deal. But you don't have to compromise. When we enter the arena, any arena, we become part of the solution and move our nation forward. Overcome the bad with good. The mob will try to torch us no matter what we do, so we might as well go for what we believe in.

When you find yourself tempted to criticize your local, state, or federal government, take that energy forward. Step into the arena yourself and call your representative. Attend a meeting. Place a campaign sign in your yard. Or maybe even send a donation to someone who is working to move America forward.

As my dad always told me, "We don't complain about things; we fix them."

THREE

BREAKERS AND BUILDERS

Look, Trump's not a conservative. [. . .] He doesn't
think in classical liberal-conservative terms.
—PAUL RYAN, DECEMBER 13, 2023[1]

Our country is in serious trouble. We don't have
victories anymore.
—CANDIDATE DONALD TRUMP, JUNE 2015[2]

My dad was someone few truly understood. He could
be busy farming ten thousand acres, but if there
was another two thousand acres available to rent
and farm, he'd try to make it work. Sometimes, semitrucks
would pull into the ranch and deliver a breed of cattle I'd
never heard of. My siblings and I were informed that we were
going to raise them and see how they did. The largest corn
planter equipment on the market planted twelve rows at one
time, but for Dad, that didn't seem to be fast enough. So he
invented a way to attach two twelve-row planters together and

be even more productive. "We're burnin' daylight," he would often say, quoting John Wayne.

That was the environment I grew up in—always questioning limitations and believing in new possibilities.

In 2015, I was serving in Congress, and I initially supported Marco Rubio's run for president—even going to Iowa and talking with farmers and ranchers on his behalf. Marco was young and energetic, and I'd gotten to know him pretty well when we worked on paid family leave policy in Congress—he as a US senator, and I as a representative. We held the same values and agreed on farm policy. He had a powerful story to share with the American people and could lead on tough issues.

After Marco dropped out of the race, supporting Trump was not a difficult decision. Trump's renegade spirit had always resonated with me. It reminded me of some members of my family. But many people in my state and across the nation were not so convinced. Mike Rounds, our former governor, did not support Donald Trump. Even after the Republican primary, when the race came down to Trump and Hillary Clinton, and after the infamous *Access Hollywood* videotape was revealed, my entire delegation in South Dakota was not supportive of Trump. Every one of the Republicans called for Trump to drop out of the race, which meant they believed Hillary Clinton should be the next president. *Amazing, right?*

As a candidate, Donald Trump did everything that the consultants had told me *not* to do. He did what everyone in Washington was *afraid* to do. He did some things I would *never* do. But he was running, he was working, he was doing, and he was speaking clearly.

And America was listening.

SIGNS OF LIFE

The 2016 election was just weeks away, and most of the experts were certain Hillary would prevail. But, as usual, those "experts" (or, as Trump would call them, the *geniuses*) were not listening beyond the Beltway. One weekend in October 2016 I flew from DC to Nashville to see my daughter. She had driven there to deliver some custom firepits that my brother had built and needed delivered to the area. A friend rode along with her from South Dakota to Nashville with the heavily loaded pickup and flatbed trailer, but she needed company for the drive home. So I caught a flight to Nashville after a long week in DC so we could drive home together. That eighteen-hour drive erased any doubt about the eruption breaking across our nation.

Actually, signs of the eruption appeared almost immediately. We got to the truck and flatbed that I had someone else hook up and get ready for us to take off early in the morning. I made the mistake of not checking the hitch, but just jumped into the truck at six a.m. and hit the interstate headed out of Nashville. About ten minutes into the drive, going seventy miles per hour in eight lanes of crowded traffic, we hit a bump, and the trailer came unhitched. The heavy hitch slammed onto the asphalt, sparks flew everywhere, and the back end of the truck fishtailed almost out of control!

I struggled to get the rig slowed down without slamming the trailer into the tailgate of the pickup and without breaking the safety chains holding the trailer to the pickup. Those chains were the only thing keeping that trailer from running across traffic and surely hurting dozens of people.

I eventually got the rig slowed down, pulled over to the side of the freeway, and assessed the damage. My daughter

Kass and I were both shaken and just stood there as thousands of people rushed by in their vehicles, oblivious to the destruction we had all just avoided. "Gosh, Kass, we could have killed so many people," I said shaking my head in disbelief. "I know," she said, in agreement. "Thank God we didn't." What a miracle.

We got the jack out of the pickup, jacked up the hitch, hooked up the trailer again—securely, this time—checked the safety chains for integrity, and took off. I'd hitched and unhitched trailers thousands of times in my life, but this was the most thoroughly I've ever done it. We were silent for the next few hours, thinking about what could have been and not knowing what to say. Eventually we relaxed and started to chat and catch up with each other about our week.

We stopped for breakfast, fueled up, and started to notice something kind of strange. Almost all the truckers we passed on the interstate or saw at the truck stops wore Make America Great Again (MAGA) red hats. Most folks driving trucks, utility vehicles, or family cars had MAGA bumper stickers or shirts, or American flags. Even though I'd been campaigning for Donald Trump and believed he could win, the level of support we witnessed in the heartland surprised me.

The prevailing narratives back in DC were "Everyone hates Trump" and "Hillary really wouldn't be so bad." And these sentiments were coming from many Republicans! They were waiting for him to fail so politics could go back to normal. But hour after hour on the roads, passing through cities, small towns, and rural areas, you could see that something about Trump was resonating with the American people. They were all in. I knew it then for sure: he was going to win. It didn't matter what the politicians, political experts, and media were saying. He had the hearts of the American people, and they proudly displayed their loyalty.

This experience confirmed my hunch—a deep conviction, actually—that this country was not going back to the way things were. Trump always was, and still is, a fighter. And someone fighting for you inspires loyalty. I'd never seen a politician earn that kind of loyalty before. Even eighty-something-year-old church ladies, who would have been greatly offended if I let a cuss word slip, overlooked his style and colorful vocabulary and cheered him on.

Donald Trump changed the national conversation and didn't just rewrite the political playbook—he obliterated it. His approach won voters' hearts, confirmed that what they believed was worthy of attention, and gave them confidence to speak up. Trump's example made it clear that elected leaders could—and should—be bolder. Personally, I gave myself permission to be even more unfiltered in Congress, and playing a small part in the 2016 election emboldened me to run for governor. I stood up for Trump in our state when no other statewide elected official would. And I was the only female member of the delegation. This made me a target, but it also made me stronger.

Some people try to emulate President Trump without success. They seem unaware of what authenticity looks like—the power of conviction, forged over many years of action. Instead, they take the low, thoughtless road of being verbal bomb throwers. There's a world of difference. And those fakers are so obvious, it's almost sad to watch them try to imitate his style without the substance to back it up.

We all need to speak boldly, but our actions must speak even louder.

BEFORE AND AFTER

The first time in US history a person was elected president who wasn't a military general or a previously elected official was 2016. This fact alone, that any office in this nation could be won by a complete outsider, was a game changer. But there was more to it than just that.

You see, somehow people were okay with the fact that Donald Trump was successful and rich. Typically, if you are going to run for elected office and you want to persuade everyday Americans that you are the right guy (or gal) to work for them, you don't announce your candidacy by riding down a golden escalator, right?

I remember watching the news coverage of Trump announcing his candidacy for president of the United States by floating down that escalator in his opulent New York City skyscraper and thinking, *How is this going to work?* (Most people would think there are only two escalators in the entire state of South Dakota!) The average citizen doesn't use an escalator in their day-to-day activities in most of the country.

A candidate usually tries to make big announcements by looking like an average constituent, wearing blue jeans or casual clothes, or by picking a location that makes them seem concerned about their community, like a factory or sports arena. But not Trump. He decided to be himself. He embraced his lifestyle and put it on full display for the world to see. It was a show to some of us, but not to him. He was successful and proud of it—and he knew how to Make America Great Again. It was probably the most unrelatable event for the average American, but we loved it! And after that announcement, small donations from blue-collar folks poured in.

His showmanship was very different from what politicians were told to do. "Act humble, be relatable . . . and normal" is what the experts say. And why is this advice given? In most cases it's because the candidate actually needs to act. That's the difference between most politicians and President Trump. Most politicians think they are better than other people— smarter, with broader experience or a more elite education. He really doesn't think he's better than anyone else. He values everyone. That's why so many people who have worked for him and his family for years are so loyal to him; he truly cares about them and the work that they do. He's full of surprises too.

In some funny ways, I see similarities between Trump and my granddaughter, Miss Addie (that's what I call her). She's almost three years old and, in my unbiased view, one of the most brilliant human beings I've ever met (tied for first place with my grandson, of course!). I love to watch her figure things out, in ways that grown-ups like me would never consider, because that's just how we've always done things. The surprising way she decided to neatly stack her little shoes by the door is just one example that makes me smile: one behind the other. Brilliant. Why didn't I ever think to do it that way?

And beyond this quality, she has no concept of trying to please people or acting in ways that aren't completely real for her. She's quite unpredictable, and I'm completely enamored with everything she does. She has her own mind and is engaging and opinionated. She's never fake, but I can see her studying other people to see if they are. It doesn't take her long to size someone up and determine if she wants to spend more time with them. It's refreshing and exactly what this world needs more of. I'm also blessed with a one-year-old grandson named Branch, and we have another grandchild on the way too! I can't wait to watch them grow up and learn from them. And, of course, spoil them, as all grandmas do.

BETH! I'VE BEEN WAITING TO MEET YOU

In my first book, I introduced you to my wonderful friend Beth, who quit her job to campaign with me when I first ran for Congress in 2010. She's in her sixties, short of stature, and tough. But she's a dynamo with a heart of gold. When I was first elected governor in 2018 and invited to one of my first meetings in the White House with several other governors and leaders, I invited her to join me and take in the experience, even though she hadn't done a lot of out-of-state travel and fancy trips were simply not her thing.

At the White House meeting, I was seated next to President Trump. One by one the other elected officials greeted the president and presented their requests. I happened to be the final governor to speak in the meeting, so I was brief and direct. I asked for fireworks at Mount Rushmore, trade agreement negotiation language, and for a Minuteman missile. (From that day forward, President Trump was committed to helping me secure all for our state.)

Long story short, we finally were allowed to have a fireworks celebration on July 3, 2020, and the trade negotiation concerns were addressed, but we're still waiting for that missile to be on display at our national historic site where nuclear weapons were once poised. Apparently, missiles aren't that easy to get released from museums and are in short supply these days.

As the formalities of that meeting concluded, President Trump and I chatted about how things were going in South

Dakota and for him, while others made their way out of the room. I decided to ask the president for one more favor. "Mr. President, I've got a staffer with me who loves you so much. She's worked with me for many years and is one of my dearest friends. Could she meet you and just say hi?"

"Bring her in!" he instantly responded, much to the displeasure of his team. They were, after all, trying to keep him on schedule. "Bring her into the Oval Office, and we can talk and take a picture, too," he added.

The president's staffer motioned quickly to me, and I jumped out of my chair and followed him out into the hallway to find the crowded room where all the other staffers were waiting. He reminded me over and over again how short this meeting needed to be because of the other commitments the president had that day. I nodded and assured him we would be brief.

We flung open the door to the room and almost fifty pairs of eyes swung toward us, looking to see who might be finally coming into the hold room. "Beth! Are you in here?" I asked. There was no sign of her five-foot-two frame in all the chaos. Then the president's team chimed in: "Where's Beth?!" Finally, at the back of the room we saw a little head pop up from where she had been sitting in the corner. Her eyes were wide as I motioned for her to come quickly. She weaved her way through the room, and I could tell she was terrified.

"You need to come with me," I yelled over all the chatter.

"Now!" echoed the president's body man.

As we scurried down the hallway, she asked, "What's going on? Am I in trouble?"

"Oh no, you're not in trouble," I assured her.

"But I was on my phone," she said. "I don't think I was supposed to be on my phone!"

"It's fine, we just need to hurry somewhere." Finally, we made our way past the checkpoints and into the Oval Office, where the president was seated at the Resolute Desk, reviewing some papers. Beth stopped in her tracks just inside the door when she realized where she was. Then she looked up, covered her face with her hands, and started to cry. She gave me the biggest hug ever and said "I can't believe it. I can't believe I'm here."

"It's okay," I whispered. "He wants to meet you!"

Just then, he looked up and announced, "Beth, I've been waiting to meet you!" After directing two staffers to get out of the way, he continued. "Come over here, Beth." And so began a visit that lasted over twenty minutes and included a terrific photo.

Most people don't dare touch the president when they stand next to him or shake his hand unless he offers. But by the time that visit was over, President Trump and Beth were such good friends that the picture tells the story. There sits President Trump at his desk in the Oval Office, and Beth standing beside him, her hands on his shoulders, just like lifelong friends.

The moment was so meaningful, and Beth has never shared the photo publicly. She told me that the memory was so perfect that she just doesn't want to take the chance that someone would say something that would diminish it in her mind. It was a moment just for her to cherish. I totally understand.

You see, Beth was not born into wealth. She has worked hard for everything in her life and has a beautiful family. She's gone through incredible challenges and come out stronger. Beth never quits and always cheers people on by telling them "You are a great American!" She loves our country, and she loves anyone who fights for it. Her life hasn't been easy, but she never expected it to be. For me, being a small part of arranging that meeting was an absolute honor and exactly why I do this job: to create opportunities for everyone to pursue their dream and realize it.

In the meeting with the other governors, I had watched as Trump often became bored with the endless requests and posturing. He wasn't difficult to read. (My granddaughter would have read the room in three minutes. Just sayin'.) He knows when people are trying to sound smart, impress him, or just give a speech in front of other people to look important. The president of the United States sat through that meeting and then took the time to meet with my friend, despite the objections of his staff, and you'll never make me believe he didn't enjoy every minute of the conversation. And he certainly didn't think he was better than her.

GET OUT
Politicians can keep trying to fake it, but people will see through them—now more than ever. It's safe to say that most people aren't looking for perfection in their leaders, and personally, I'm glad. We don't need to be perfect, but we must never be fake.

If you're an elected official and you think you're better than someone else in this country, *please resign!*

Quit right now, and don't run again.

You're not who we need to move this country forward.

While I'm at it, please stop telling the people you represent how "tirelessly" you've been working for them. Only politicians use that word, and it's a lie. I hate that word. Have you ever heard a school bus driver say, "I've been tirelessly driving these kids for thirty years." Of course not, even though they have actually been working hard in their community.

By the way, if right now you're thinking that your job as an elected official is more important or more challenging than that of a bus driver, you are officially the problem. If there's one person you think you're better than, you are not the kind of person that we need to help this country. Americans shouldn't have to waste our time on you anymore. The problem is, politics is full of people like that.

GET IN

The election results of 2016 tell us that anyone can enter the arena and win. We don't have to "wait our turn" to serve. If you think you'd do a good job, you should get in and run. When I was considering a run for governor, many people told me "It's not your turn. We've already decided who the next governor is going to be." But, crazy as it seemed, I thought I could do better than the man they picked. South Dakota is like a small town in many ways. Everybody knows everybody—which is a mixed blessing. And there are just a few people who have pulled the strings for many years.

So, I decided that I didn't need to bow out just because the few dozen, unappointed deciders told me I should. I simply needed thousands of Beths, and I actually prefer it that way.

The 2016 election proved that the people can still rule. Grassroots support can overrule the establishment. Small donors can make an impact. In October 2020, during COVID, I posted what I thought was a funny video about how we do social distancing in South Dakota—we go hunting. I was in a field and shot a pheasant . . . on the third attempt. "Less

COVID, more hunting," I said. It was intended as a joke, mocking myself and my poor shooting skills. It was embarrassing that it took me three shots to kill that bird. But I had obviously spent too much time that year dealing with COVID, crises, decisions, press conferences, and running our state.

That video horrified the legacy media but turned out to be one of the best ways to draw attention, and much-needed funds, to our campaign. (Yes, I'm talking about money again, but that's a part of winning against the political machine.) People made T-shirts and hats imprinted with "Less COVID, More Hunting." Hunters all over the state, along with Beths and Bobs around the country, got the message. Spend more time outdoors, together, and stop politicizing a pandemic that had mutated into a socialist agenda. America was all in for "Less COVID, more hunting!" And I loved it.[3]

(While we're talking about videos, my mom recently won a regional Telly Award for her work on "Get the Word Out" in the category of Best Use of Comedy. A Telly is like an advertising agency equivalent of a Grammy. Go, Mom!)

Another legacy of the 2016 election was the rise of the businessman in elections. Look at who was elected as governors: Bill Lee in Tennessee, Doug Burgum in North Dakota, Glenn Youngkin in Virginia, and Greg Gianforte in Montana. Like me, these guys were CEOs of their companies and ran on the idea of being the CEO of their state. Trump made it okay to be successful in business, as long as the candidate was focused on the people of their state. And I happen to believe that these governors took a page from the president's playbook on campaigning boldly, regardless of their level of support for him.

BREAKERS AND BUILDERS

Donald Trump was, and is, a bull in a china shop. There's still so much wrong with politics, and it needs more breaking. But what comes next?

The Republican Party is divided nationally, and in our state and local parties as well. South Dakota's GOP Convention in 2022 was an embarrassment. It was a three-day event that consisted of more Republicans attacking Republicans than Republicans contrasting themselves to socialist Democrats and their extreme party platform. A few months after that convention, I had conversations with our congressional delegation and asked them for help fixing the division within our state party. They were reluctant, not wanting to invest needed funds and not certain who could bring any sense of order to the chaos and deal with the outright vitriol of some within the party.

Our senior US senator, John Thune, suggested that maybe we should just let it go—don't try to save or fix the county parties around our state at that moment. Let them break, and then in a few years it will reset.

I must admit that I was discouraged by the suggestion, because I felt a responsibility to bring the party together and unify. So I went to work. I recruited a new chairman, funded an executive director, and helped raise the needed money by hosting events, investing campaign funds, and asking supporters to help them get the legal advice and structure that would right the ship and bring people together. I even asked our presidential candidates to come to South Dakota and hold rallies to raise money for the party. President Trump came, and we held a fantastic event in Rapid City that was sold out in hours. But we still had an outspoken group of

Republican Party members who focused on beating up on each other rather than making our case to the people we served. I was baffled at what they thought they were accomplishing.

I've always supported the Republican Party at all levels: towns, county, state, and national. But more and more I wonder if John Thune was right. I'm okay with Trump breaking the national model and the Republican Party. I believe common sense still rules, but the swamp oozes into every low-lying part of this country.

When it comes to our states and communities, perhaps the same holds true. Maybe real forward progress will never come from those already in the system, even those who are trying to bring unity. Now I think perhaps a breaking needs to happen in order for hard lessons to be learned. And it's going to take some farmers, teachers, businesspeople, moms, law enforcement, and everyday folks (like you) to step up and be a part of the solution.

Some say it can't get any worse. Well, maybe it needs to in order to wake up those who will finally decide to be all in for this country.

LET'S DO THE IMPOSSIBLE—AGAIN

The best gift my dad and mom ever gave us was impossible things to do. I remember the chores they would give me. I'd think, *there's no way I can do that!* But when I actually accomplished the task, I had the confidence to take on the next bigger challenge. Our parents were raising their children to become problem solvers.

Challenges are not bad—they prepare us for the future. Maybe the consequences of the 2020 election are preparing us for bigger challenges. And we're going to have to pull together to meet those challenges.

There are breakers, and there are builders. We need people to keep breaking what's not working. Finish the job. Expose the corruption, manipulation, and dysfunction. Those with authority in government need to step up and do what's right—regardless of the cost to their comfy careers. You and I, with the power of our voice and our vote, can also tear down what's broken. But then we must rebuild. And ensure that through the breaking, that we don't break the American spirit. Instead, we must inspire.

Republican leaders, don't let us down again. Honestly, you're like the *Peanuts* cartoon where Lucy keeps pulling the football away from Charlie Brown. Every time we think we have a chance to make a field goal, you let us down. We're optimistic, but we have no patience for you anymore.

We need builders, too. I'm looking for "surprise" people who step in and shake things up. Donald Trump was a breaker and a builder, but one person can't rebuild an entire nation. Just look at how much that he built that has fallen into the swamp since 2020. It's staggering how far back we've come in just a few years. We need you to be a builder.

2020

The 2020 election changed our nation, too. Sadly, we became further divided. Candidate Joe Biden talked about bringing everyone together. That talk lasted about one minute after the inauguration. And the media loved it. They perpetuated the division. You may remember that prior to the election CNN highlighted a daily tracker of how many people died of COVID. It was a top headline every hour. You might also remember that as soon as Biden got elected, those statistics faded into the distance. The tracker stopped almost immediately.

Trump exposed the swamp—some of it anyway—and after Biden was elected, the bureaucrats scrambled to protect it like a national park.

Anyone who loves the status quo hates to be questioned. When political predictability is threatened by a disruptor, the knives come out. As someone who was in Congress from 2011 to 2019, I can tell you that a number of people in Washington felt personally insulted that someone who had never held public office could win the highest office in the land. The insiders of both parties believed Trump hadn't "put his time in." *Thank God he didn't.*

I believe most Americans, on some level, are happy that Trump shook things up. To someone unfamiliar with American politics, the story of a brash billionaire being relatable to everyday people might sound unbelievable. To me, Donald Trump talks like normal people talk, like my friends and neighbors talk—not like people in DC talk.

He was relentlessly attacked for personal failures—and fictional ones—but stayed in the race and never wavered. That aspect of the man was inspirational. Yes, I am inspired by his shortcomings. Like Teddy Roosevelt said, "there is no effort without error and shortcoming."[4] Nobody has a perfect life or perfect relationships in every season of life, but professional politicians pretend to. Trump wasn't pretending, and that quality connected with people.

In 2020, I went to twenty-seven states campaigning for him. He has my full endorsement in 2024. In the past four years, so much of what Trump accomplished has been threatened. The DC monster does not want change. And we still need someone who will tell the truth and reform our nation.

The United States of America needs dramatic change to continue in a way that's only possible from the White House. And we also need change agents in every level of government, in every county and town and school.

GOOD NEWS

When we think back on our best friends and best moments in life, we remember the people who bring a reason to smile every day. This reminds me of one of my favorite scriptures: "How beautiful on the mountains are the feet of those who bring good news, who proclaim peace, who bring good tidings, who proclaim salvation, who say to Zion, 'Your God reigns!'" (Isaiah 52:7 NIV).

I picture someone running toward me, appearing over a mountain, with good news, proclaiming or even shouting "Peace," and announcing news of happiness. They're smiling, and it makes me smile. Even seeing their feet running to us with the exciting news can be described as beautiful. I so love that vision.

Forget politics for a minute. This is what we need in our land. And this is the kind of person I strive to be—someone who brings encouragement and a smile from the heart.

Tony Venhuizen was my chief of staff during COVID, and we didn't always agree on everything. He had also been chief of staff to the former governor. But what I loved about working with him was that even in the midst of tense conversations, he'd say something lighthearted or witty and release the tension in the room. It was such a blessing.

For me, that's a lesson I want to learn from 2016, 2020, and today. There's a lot of serious work needed to build and move forward, but we don't have to take ourselves so seriously that we forget to be human.

STEP FORWARD

Regardless of your personal feelings, what stands out to you from watching Donald Trump as a candidate and as president?

What have you learned about the establishment in the past few years? Most important, what are you going to do to be part of the solution?

Personally, whether I'm in elected office or not, I decided years ago to trust my convictions more, to speak my mind more, and to utterly ignore the establishment.

I believe the establishment's main goal is to silence good people. And we've seen that they'll use any means necessary to accomplish this goal. We won't be silenced anymore. But we also need to show up.

We get to pick who represents us, not the pundits, consultants, and swampy insiders.

FOUR

GAS STATIONS, GUN SHOPS, AND GOVERNORS

And first of all, I think marijuana is going to pass this year. I think we're going to have a new thing to tax. Some good friend of mine from the past said, 'We don't need to tax things more. We need more things to tax.' And I think we're going to get one.

—JAMIE SMITH, DEMOCRAT CHALLENGER FOR GOVERNOR OF SOUTH DAKOTA, OCTOBER 2022[1]

The trouble with our liberal friends is not that they're ignorant; it's just that they know so much that isn't so.

—RONALD REAGAN[2]

Y ou can tell a lot about somebody by what's on their desk. When I walk into someone's office, I always take note of the items and quotes they keep close to them.

If you saw my desk, you'd see my dad's Bible next to one of our ranch's original branding irons. I have various photos of my family, and a big tub of cotton candy. I treasure the clock that former South Dakota chief justice David Gilbertson gave me. Because he's a clock collector, the gift meant a lot. Justice Gilbertson was also a mentor. Most suspect he was a Democrat, but nobody really cares—because he was such a good chief justice of our Supreme Court.

Many guests wonder why there's a teacher's bell on my desk. When I first became governor, whenever I had questions for staff, I'd wander around the capitol halls looking for the particular person. One day in a meeting, one of the state attorneys presented me with the vintage bell, and said, "Governor, you don't have to track us down when you have a question—just call us! Or ring this bell, and we'll be here." Point taken. But I still prefer to walk down the hall and have an eye-to-eye conversation.

After a particularly trying season in my first term, someone gave me a plaque that reads "My life feels like a test I didn't study for." That pretty much sums up every day at the capitol. Along with those humbling words sits another plaque—a gift from my dear uncle, who happens to be very much a Democrat. When I was first elected to Congress he gave it to me as a reminder that "Well-behaved women rarely make history."[3]

Those words also remind me that social media rants and sound bites don't make history. Accomplishments do.

THE BOMB THROWERS

There's a stark difference between breaking the unspoken rules and throwing political bombs. The difference is substance: *are there actual solutions being proposed?* Bomb throwers rarely offer practical plans of action. They are vocal about what—and who—they're against, but weirdly quiet about what they're for and how to accomplish it.

As we read in the Bible, the apostle Paul wrote to Christians who were living in a very hostile environment in Rome, "Do not be overcome by evil, but overcome evil with good" (Romans 12:21 NIV).

It's so easy to criticize the establishment of both parties and toss verbal grenades. Sadly, social media often rewards these stunts. We'll only move forward when we propose solutions, build coalitions, and see results. In Congress, it's too easy to make news by throwing stones and deflecting blame. But when you are governor, people look to you for results.

RESULTS

At the governor's residence, there's a sign on one of my end tables: "Underestimate me. That'll be fun."

As I write this, South Dakota has the nation's number one economy when you look at a combination of unemployment, GDP growth, and rising personal incomes.[4]

We had the fewest business closures from the pandemic, the fewest number of hours lost by workers, and the least amount of wages lost by employees.[5] Over the last three years, our people's incomes have grown by 21 percent, the most of any state, and personal income is up 30 percent since I became governor.[6]

When President Trump offered elevated unemployment benefits during COVID, I was the only governor in the country who turned him down. I essentially said, "Thank you, Mr. President, for the flexibility, but we don't need it. Our people want to work." Today we have fewer than seven hundred people in our entire state on unemployment.[7]

In recent years, because of our thriving economy, South Dakota's sales tax revenues have reached historic levels, along with a record budget surplus—even though our state has *no* income taxes (corporate or personal) and no personal property taxes. And our sales tax rate is just 4.2 percent. By the way, I don't propose conservative spending in our budgets because our state's economy is weak, but because we're strong and want to stay that way.

Since I have been governor, we've paid off debt and put historic amounts into trust funds and reserves. We've repaired dams and built railroads, roads, and bridges. I had a vision to bring high-speed internet to every corner of the state during my years as governor, and we fully funded the project in just one year. South Dakota has a AAA credit rating and a fully funded pension plan.

We have a constitutional requirement to balance our state budget. Yes. That's a real thing.

Through all of this, South Dakota has emerged as the best example of freedom in the nation. And I gladly give credit where it is due—to the people of South Dakota. Most of the great work we've accomplished together has been the result of government getting out of the way. We have become the starkest contrast to Joe Biden's America. Joe Biden's America wants to take away your freedoms, like the right to keep and bear arms.

South Dakota is setting the bar for defending the Second Amendment. The very first bill I signed into law when I became governor was constitutional carry, which means you don't need a license to carry a concealed weapon. And in 2023 South Dakota became the first state to waive all fees (including your federal background check) for concealed carry permits. In our state, it won't cost you a penny to exercise your Second Amendment rights.

We banned critical race theory from our universities. Governments are instituted among men to preserve our unalienable rights—among these are life, liberty, and the pursuit of happiness. And *life* comes first. In South Dakota, we are saving unborn lives and helping mothers in crisis. We're making sure that moms know what help is available to them, no matter what situation they may face.

South Dakota is the best example of freedom working. And that's why the left attacks us or tries to dismiss us. We have led the nation in housing developments. Women-owned businesses are thriving at rates among the best in the nation. People are moving to South Dakota by the thousands—but there's plenty of room for you.[8]

Because I served in Washington, I'm constantly giving members of Congress ideas for important legislation that helps our state—and our nation. (You're welcome, America!) Recently, I asked several representatives about a challenge with our pension fund. A certain brokerage's emerging markets fund still classified China as an emerging market. Everybody in the world, with the exception of people in DC, knows that China does not qualify—and they take advantage of that designation. I recently suggested a bill that would not allow these investment firms to call China an emerging market and would allow states to divest from Chinese investments without being in violation of their fiduciary responsibility. The bill was introduced by South Dakota's at-large congressman, Dusty Johnson, in November. No action has taken place on the bill just yet, but stay tuned.[9]

There are so many ways governors and Congress can work together. It simply takes knowledge of who to contact and the desire to have conversations.

When leaders make a case for change and take action, the establishment takes notice. I led the charge to ban TikTok on government devices, and within weeks we saw dozens of states, Republican and Democrat, follow suit. I pushed the federal government and the Biden administration to do the same, called them out on the threat of the communist Chinese spy app, and eventually they did. (With a few notable exceptions. *I'm talking to you, Kamala.*)

GLOBAL PERSPECTIVE

In Congress I saw so much waste in federal government spending—reckless spending overseas, at the national level, and in how funds were allocated to states. I'll spare you the details here, but trust me, it's even worse than you imagine. When I became governor I knew how to make sure those funds were used effectively, in ways that actually produce a return on the investment.

My experience also helped me build a huge network of helpful contacts in DC. I can pick up the phone and call people who help us move crucial improvements forward. Building solid relationships is key, and I'm not talking about cronies or compromise. Even though you may fundamentally disagree with someone, having the ability to talk with them directly is a powerful tool that many elected officials overlook.

For example, the United States secretary of agriculture, Tom Vilsack, was secretary during the Obama administration, and I worked closely with him on the 2013 farm bill and conservation programs while I was in Congress. He has returned again to the role in the Biden administration, and as governor I've been able to leverage this productive relationship to weigh in on policies affecting our state. My knowledge of the programs and how I can best use the flexibility in them to help my farmers and ranchers, and the relationship I have with the secretary have benefited the people in our state.

The same is true when it comes to international relationships. Governors—effective ones, anyway—lead their state in trade negotiations and open up new opportunities. As a congresswoman and governor, I've met with Chinese president Xi Jingping, the king and princes of Saudi Arabia, North Korean president Kim Jong Un, the king of Jordan, South Korean president Lee Myung-bak, Israeli prime minister Benjamin Netanyahu, UK prime minister Boris Johnson, Egyptian president Abdel Fattah al-Sisi, and many more.

Through my tenure on the House Armed Services Committee, I had the chance to travel to many countries to meet with world leaders—some who wanted our help, and some who didn't. I remember when I met with North Korean dictator Kim Jong Un. I'm sure he underestimated me, having no clue about my experience staring down little tyrants (I'd been a children's pastor, after all). Dealing with foreign leaders takes resolve, preparation, and determination. My experiences on those many foreign trips made me a better member of Congress and a stronger governor. It allowed me to hone my deal-making skills, which play a crucial role in leadership.

Today, in order to further our state's success, we send representatives all over the world. The team from the Department of Agriculture and Natural Resources has negotiated in close to a dozen countries in the past year—Malaysia, India,

Brazil, and many other South American countries. We plan our goals and track progress, because we create these trading channels that are important for the beef and soybean producers in our state, among others.

In 2023 we sent our lieutenant governor to Mexico because they instituted a new regulation that would have drastically cut imports of South Dakota beef and grain. He brought a team of business leaders to bring more light to Mexico's concerns and educate their trade negotiators on the issues. Bottom line: they came home with millions of dollars' worth of business, based on South Dakota values. These international trade agreements build connections that do more than grow our economy. In a very real way, they strengthen human relationships and foster peace.

If your governor isn't personally involved in opening up more exports from your state, give them a copy of this book and tell them they can call me. (And please read the appendices, based on my 2023 budget speech and 2024 State of the State address, for a real eye-opener on what's possible when freedom leads.)

BROKEN EXECUTIVE BRANCHES

To paraphrase Milton Friedman, when the government thinks it's the answer to everyone's problems, it becomes a problem for everyone. In any leadership position, it's easy to fall into the mindset that every issue that comes to your attention requires your help. This posture puts you on the defense as opposed to in a forward focus.

A backward government is always playing defense and responding to the status quo. That's the way South Dakota operated for many years. Lobbyists were deciding what bills passed and what bills didn't. How does this happen? Because there was a vacuum of public involvement.

The leaders of our state were not doing enough to educate their citizens and remind them that *they* were often the solution—not government.

Here's how it goes. There's a problem. The knee-jerk reaction from elected officials and bureaucrats is "What will we do to address this? Let's allocate money, create a new department, hire personnel, commission three new feasibility studies, and see what we can do!" This approach enshrines the problem for all eternity.

We still don't do everything right in my state, but we're definitely moving things in the right direction.

Instead of creating new layers of government, we've eliminated or consolidated departments and boards. South Dakota had twenty-one cabinet secretaries, and so far we're down to nineteen, and counting. For example, we had a Department of Natural Resources and a Department of Agriculture. So I put them together. Common sense, right? Why would you not want to have the water biologists and people who test our water quality sitting right next to the folks who approve the permits for feedlots?

When you work alongside someone, you can more easily find simple solutions. Accountability increases, and so does efficiency.

The halls of power in the executive and legislative branches are crawling with lobbyists, advocating for the people who pay them. But who is roaming the halls on *your* behalf? Almost no one. You have a life. Your time and energy are limited. You want less government. That's why we must elect leaders who really care about you and will fight the status quo.

GAS STATIONS AND GUN SHOPS

Loud voices aren't necessarily more important; they're just more distracting. I have to remind myself and my team of this almost every day.

What helps me keep my perspective is prioritizing time spent in gas stations and gun shops. A few months ago I, along with a couple staffers, got on our motorcycles and went for a ride. We stopped in little cafés, had a piece of pie, and had lots of conversations with South Dakotans.

Nobody expects the governor to ride in, unannounced, and ask questions. One lady asked me, "Have you ever been to Presho before?"

"I'm actually here a lot," I replied. "Every few weeks."

That day we had several informative conversations, because I simply sat down at a table and listened. (A group of folks even offered to pray for me. It was a very special moment.)

While we were chatting with people at another café, a teacher stopped in to pick up cookies for her class. I learned she was buying treats for a little girl's birthday the next day. She knew her parents would forget, and every other kid brought treats on their birthdays. So there she was, going the extra mile for her students and her community.

These are not campaign stops or designed to win me more votes. This is what it takes to be a leader, and it is part of the job as governor. It happens to be one of the best parts, and absolutely essential for keeping perspective. You don't experience amazing stuff like that unless you get out of your office and talk with people.

And I hope it also makes a difference for the people we met. Many times following road trips like this, I hear from others in the community. "I heard you met my sister at the café. Sorry I missed you, but maybe I'll see you next time— Thanks so much!" Word travels fast in small towns, and when you listen, people notice.

YOUR VOICE ACTUALLY COUNTS

The main message I hope people understand when I'm hanging out in gun shops and gas stations is that their voice really does matter. I believe that one of the main reasons more people don't contact their elected officials is because they've bought the lie that their voice doesn't really matter. *Why bother to call the office and tell them I support this or that? Why send an email? Nobody cares.*

Here's the truth, in my administration, anyway: if we get three or four phone calls, I immediately know we have an issue. I tell people all the time, you'd be surprised at how little it takes for us to pay attention. I make sure the ladies at the front desk aren't just invited to our weekly staff meeting but actively participate. They are often the first line of communication and hear about issues long before the rest of the staff. Their job is one of the most critical in our office, and that's why I've given them the power to resolve simple issues for people—without a committee or red tape.

Leadership is about focusing on people, not problems.

WHY NOT?

When ideas are proposed, I quickly stopped asking why we *would* do something and started asking why we *wouldn't* do it. This approach fundamentally changes the conversation and the outcome.

If somebody proposed a bill that allows us to sell our lumber to Canada, instead of asking "Why would we do that?" the question "Why wouldn't we?" is much more productive.

Often, there are many reasons why we wouldn't adopt an idea. Maybe it's not the government's job; maybe it's unconstitutional. But if there's not a good reason why we wouldn't, then maybe we should figure out how to get it done.

A forward-focused executive branch pushes opportunity constantly. That's how we stay on the offense and make progress. What really bothers me, and what we strive to avoid, are missed opportunities.

MODERATELY AND CONSERVATIVELY?

What's my number one piece of advice to anyone stepping into the area of politics? Thanks for asking. *Talk moderately so you can govern conservatively.*

Let's face it, Republicans screw this up, a lot. Candidates talk like crazy people, make wild claims, and offer big promises. And they lose. Of course, there are some crazy candidates, but I'm not talking about them. This is about good folks who choose the wide path of bomb throwing and parroting whatever's on social media, as opposed to speaking rationally and humbly offering solutions.

Friends, we need to win. If we don't win, we don't govern. But here's what so many folks miss: if you can't have a friendly conversation with a teacher at a café or the cashier at the gas station, please don't run for office—even for dog catcher.

At the same time, we can, and must, hold true to our core beliefs. This often means that when something isn't right, we say so—regardless of party affiliation. It's the only way to long-term success and the only way to look yourself in the mirror with a clear conscience. This was put to the test a few years ago.

THE NARROW ROAD

On the night of September 12, 2020, Jason Ravnsborg, the Republican attorney general of South Dakota, was driving home alone from a Lincoln Day dinner. The ensuing investigation revealed he was reading an article on his cell phone when his car hit a man who was walking on the side of the roadway. Ravnsborg called 911, informed the dispatcher of who he was, and then reported he hit "something."

The local sheriff responded to the scene; together, they walked the general area and supposedly didn't see anything. Ravnsborg's car was so badly damaged that it couldn't be driven. Accordingly, the sheriff then gave Ravnsborg his personal vehicle to drive home. Does any of this make sense to you so far?

The following day, Ravnsborg and his chief of staff returned to the accident site because he claimed he wanted to see if he could find what he hit. It was then when Ravnsborg pointed out a human body to his colleague. He did not call 911. Instead, he casually drove to the sheriff's home to return the borrowed vehicle and proceeded to tell the sheriff about his gruesome discovery.

As the investigation unfolded, some disturbing facts arose.

Within the first twenty-four hours, I held a press conference announcing a further investigation into the matter. It became more and more clear to me that Ravnsborg was not being honest about what transpired that night. What is not in dispute is that the vehicle he was driving struck and killed a man and Ravnsborg left the scene, only to return the next day to find the man's body in a ditch on the side of the road.

Investigators called in from a neighboring state to prevent any conflict of interest determined that the deceased man's head had gone through the car's windshield. As a matter of fact, the deceased's eyeglasses were found inside Ravnsborg's vehicle, which was being held at a salvage yard. Evidence further indicated the man's body was dragged by the vehicle for a considerable distance.

As these facts became known, I called for his immediate resignation, noting that it was not proper for him to remain the "top cop" in the state. There were serious questions about his conduct, his honesty in his interviews with law enforcement, his communications with subordinates, and what he did to attempt to conceal the truth about that evening.

As I've said many times, South Dakota has a strong good old boys network, and the Republican speaker of the House of Representatives was one of Ravnsborg's best buddies. This made my calling for an investigation very ugly for both of these men. Not only did Ravnsborg refuse to resign, but the Speaker of the House vigorously and publicly defended him. Realizing I wouldn't get much support from the legislative leaders to hold Ravnsborg accountable, I called for him to be impeached, which would require that all the evidence in the case be brought forth for the public to see and hear.

It sure seemed like I was the only one pushing for the truth. Many Republicans were offended that I would go after a fellow Republican. My actions were based on the facts of the case. Politics had no place here. This was about right and wrong and upholding the law, and I knew what side I was on.

My staff was concerned that the attorney general would aggressively retaliate against me. We were told that if he didn't get impeached, he was considering opening a grand jury investigation into me and my office. This was an ugly prospect for many reasons, but especially because grand juries are very different from other legal challenges. You don't get the chance to defend yourself or tell your side of the story to a grand jury.

In the end, Ravnsborg was found guilty on two counts, was removed from office, and became the first person in South Dakota history to be barred from ever running for office again. A cousin of the deceased man called the verdict "vindication."[10]

People think I never liked Jason Ravnsborg. The truth is, I did, and we helped him in his early years. To me, it didn't matter if he was a Republican or Democrat. He lied and abused his office. Transparency won the day. It was an ugly, difficult year, but we stood for the truth and justice. If something is wrong, our choice is easy.

STEP FORWARD

So many of the problems we face as conservatives are self-inflicted. Let's stop shooting our mouths off and stop shooting ourselves in the foot.

Sure, we can blame the media or liberals, but the truth is we need to be smarter, speak clearly, and tell the truth.

As famed coach Woody Hayes always said, "You win with people."

When we lead with a genuine focus on the people we serve, we can smile and say, "Underestimate us, that'll be fun."

FIVE

COVID AS A CASE STUDY

This evening, I tested positive for COVID-19. Thankfully, I
am only experiencing mild symptoms after being fully
vaccinated and twice boosted, and I encourage my fellow
Michiganders to get vaccinated and boosted, too.

—GOVERNOR GRETCHEN WHITMER, AUGUST 8, 2022[1]

*And to those concerned about what the future might hold
for you if you stay where you are right now, come to South
Dakota. The air is fresh, the people are free, and the
possibilities are endless.*

—ME, JUNE 8, 2020

The COVID-19 pandemic was a test for this country. And, as others have pointed out, we were the lab rats.

It's quite possible you came to know my name during COVID, or possibly the name the media "experts" at *Rolling Stone* magazine gave me: "the Covid Queen." From Elizabeth Warren to Rachel Maddow, night after night on national news they declared that I was reckless, irresponsible, and dangerous.

I was even parodied on *Saturday Night Live* in October 2022, after the cast and crew decided they could emerge from their dens. They parodied me as a vampire, talking with Trump in the Oval Office.[2] Some would say I'd finally made it. But the sketch was just sad. Liberals were stuck in the ditch, using fear to demonize those who disagreed with their doctrine of government control.

At one point early on in the pandemic, on a Sunday morning show, I was waiting my turn to visit with George Stephanopoulos who was interviewing then New York governor Andrew Cuomo. Before he closed out his conversation with Cuomo, he asked him a curious question about giving me some advice.[3] Yes, that Governor Cuomo—the one who, among other things, sent vulnerable seniors to their deaths in nursing homes and then tried to cover it up. Maybe George should have asked me to give advice to Governor Cuomo.

My team and I studied the science, researched the data, and talked to medical experts. But I also took it another step further: I talked to my general counsel and constitutional experts. I wanted to fully understand what authority I had—and what authority I didn't have—as governor. Because when leaders overstep their authority, especially in a time of crisis, that's how we lose our republic.

South Dakota was the only state in the nation that never once closed a single business. I never defined what an "essential business" was because I don't believe governors have the authority to tell you your business isn't essential. I never stopped people from going to church or holding meetings. I held press conferences and meetings and stood in front of my people and told them I was going to trust them. I promised to give them all the information I had and let them use personal responsibility to make the best decisions for their family and asked them to help take care of their neighbors. Pretty dangerous, huh?

Because of my experience in business, the state legislature, and in Washington, I was more prepared as governor to do the right thing for South Dakota—even when the world went nuts. We kept perspective, questioned the so-called experts, and focused on working together. There were no perfect solutions or choices. There were no victory laps—far from it. But we followed the Constitution, trusted our people, and chose to protect freedom.

As we all know, other states did enforce mandates and closures. (Although many governors from both parties are trying to rewrite history, denying they closed or mandated anything. But you know the truth.) Kids lost precious time in the classroom and suffered because of the closures. Small businesses were crippled by regulations and restrictions. Almost a million businesses closed. Hundreds of thousands of these small businesses across the country closed, forever.[4]

Several governors called me in 2020, sharing their fears and asking questions. I asked them about issues, too, but always reminded them to consider these crucial questions:

"What is the proper role of government?"

"What authorities do you have as defined by your state Constitution?"

"Does the US Constitution allow you to take that action?"

"What kind of litigation do you open your state up to if you do that and if you are wrong, who will pay the price?"

Many of these leaders had no one else around them asking these questions. They had no idea that their state could stand against the insanity and panic-driven overreach.

CHECK THEIR REFERENCES

There is always changing personnel in the White House, and I often noticed a shift in operations. I was still having meetings with the president regarding important policies. But more and more, the president would agree to help me with something, we'd shake hands, and I'd leave the office. More than once, his then chief of staff, John Kelly, would say to me various versions of "Yeah, we're not going to do that."

It was clear to me that the president did not have a team who had his same mission, and I knew this could cause us a lot of problems in the future if it continued. But I had no idea how bad it would get.

As COVID concerns grew worldwide, people were looking for daily information and leaders they could trust. The problem was that our nation hadn't faced a crisis like this in many decades. By this time in the Trump administration, the establishment had gained ground—certainly in Congress, but also inside the White House.

Let's face it, in the chaos, who would want to be the face of all things COVID? The president initially put Jared Kushner in charge of preparing the country for the pandemic, but soon it became clear that the only person in the White House who had the experience to run a full federal response to a crisis was Vice President Mike Pence. As a former governor, he had led during crisis situations in his home state of Indiana, and with his experience as a member of Congress he had knowledge about the workings of the Federal Emergency Management Agency and other agencies that would offer needed assistance. Pence officially became the COVID czar and, in the end, chose to put his trust in Dr. Anthony Fauci and Dr. Deborah Birx, among others.

I was a bit astonished to see so many leaders look to these doctors as credible experts to lead us through this unprecedented challenge. It's not that I questioned their medical résumés; I questioned how much their politics would influence their decisions. Because no one in the Trump administration wanted responsibility for this horrible situation if it went south and millions of people died, our nation's leaders turned to leftist ideologues and gave them credibility in front of the American people. It was dangerous.

Now don't get me wrong: countless people of all political persuasions were giving bad advice back then. But Dr. Fauci and Dr. Birx had been political animals their entire lives. How certain could we be that they would never let their agenda influence the advice they gave? It was 2020, after all, and the election virus had already swept the nation.

I told the vice president one day on the phone, "I do not understand why you're working with Dr. Fauci. He's ideologically opposed to what we stand for. I've watched him run around DC for years with Nancy Pelosi's crew. He's not on our team, can't be trusted, and at some point he's gonna throw us all—including the president—under the bus."

I was willing to give the czar and the experts a chance but also was determined to ask questions and do our own research. I soon found an ally in Dr. Scott Atlas, who became an invaluable resource to my executive team. He didn't tell us what to do or what to think. He sent us data points, research, and information on different approaches other countries were taking to deal with this virus. And he asked hard questions. He was a senior advisor in the White House during the pandemic, but he soon found himself isolated amongst the liberals who were really calling the shots on the nation's response.

But I found Dr. Atlas to be someone of integrity, based on the fact that he didn't let political pressure sway his informed views. He helped get truth to leaders who needed all the facts to make the best decisions.

By August of that year, as Dr. Fauci's poor advice and hypocrisy were being exposed more and more, Trump began social distancing himself from the doctor, declaring that he disagreed with him on many areas and that he "inherited him."[5] Regardless, Dr. Fauci maintained the position he was given and used it to wield a lot of power. Sadly, he seemed to enjoy the role a little too much.

In the aftermath, and unlike most of the population, people like Fauci got wealthier from the pandemic.[6] They never shed a tear over a small business, church, or restaurant that was forced to close. They perpetuated government control and pushed a Marxist socialist agenda. And they used fear to steal people's constitutional freedoms. They should never be forgiven for that.

MEANWHILE IN SOUTH DAKOTA

We paid close attention to the information and opinions coming from Washington, but we also investigated data ourselves with the help of medical professionals. Bottom line: I wanted to know what was working, what wasn't working, and why.

Other governors were letting the federal government call the shots. (I know, because I spoke to dozens of governors that year.) People were scared, and they let fear control them. I knew the citizens of my state were looking to me for guidance and information. "Do you want to shut down all the schools? Should we close every business?" My answer was always *no*, knowing that I didn't have that authority. But I was shocked at how angry local leaders got when I wouldn't do it.

They wanted me to make the hard decision to close schools, churches, and businesses so that they didn't have to make the decision at the city, county, or school district level. They would call me yelling, frustrated, and some even crying, saying, "Governor, you have to do this! I can't take this pressure!" So, I spent a lot of my time on the phone, on conference calls, and in tele-town halls with state legislators, city council members, county commissioners, and mayors. I reassured, encouraged, and explained what my position was based on. We also shared data, research, and facts so they could be confident in the decisions they were making, too.

The wonderful teams in my office had the opportunity to write a lot of the guidance for federal dollars tied to COVID—simply because there was no precedent. My former chief of staff had worked in the Treasury Department, and we built relationships with many folks in federal agencies who were charged with getting resources to the states, simply because we were proactive in asking about how we used federal dollars in the best and most efficient ways. As every state began to receive public health dollars we asked, "What's your guidance on how to use these funds?" When they answered that they did not know yet, we offered to write up suggestions for them to use, and many of them were incorporated into the final guidance that went out to every state.

In June 2020 (long before other politicians started to wake up to the harm of lockdowns and mandates), I recorded a video message for South Dakotans—and anyone else who was interested—to share some perspective and lessons learned. Here are a few special sections from that address.

OPEN FOR BUSINESS

Perhaps the most significant takeaway so far is that more freedom, not more government, is the answer. While freedom alone won't solve all of our problems, it does present a better path toward where we want to go. Freedom is a better friend of true science than government-centered and government-controlled science.

Freedom is also a best friend of innovation. It focuses our politics on persuasion and the intellectual strength of our positions, not uncontrolled coercion or the heavy hand of government. If someone is interested in the common good in all its iterations and complexities, freedom is the one and only choice.

My approach to this virus was to provide South Dakotans with all the information that I could and then trust them to exercise their freedom to make the best decision for themselves and for their families. We took a unique path: we haven't locked people up, forced businesses or churches to close, or ordered a statewide shelter in place. In return, the mainstream media has spent many hours and nearly endless column inches attacking me for that. But countless South Dakotans have thanked me for trusting them.

Recently, I was able to spend some quiet time with my family in the Black Hills, one of the most picture-perfect places on the planet. We were not alone; I've never seen so many visitors to the Black Hills in my life. License plates from every corner of this country.

While the media was attacking me, the people were watching.

As many of my peers applied a one-size-fits-all lockdown, ordinary Americans, the lifeblood of this nation, saw what we were doing, and many said, "That's exactly the way I want my government to treat me, to trust me, not dictate to me."

So, this leaves me to wonder: what does this say about the state of our media? The mainstream media attacks those who push for freedom and for people to be able to make the best decisions for their families. But politicians who take away people's freedoms and enforce lockdowns are praised and shielded from real scrutiny.

No model can actually predict the future, especially when it's based on incomplete data, and no model is capable of replacing human freedom as the best path to responding to life's risks, including this virus. That is why central planning of the economy has failed every time the government has tried it. In South Dakota, we saw modeling as a tool, and we used it to be prepared for a worst-case scenario. I thank God that the worst case hasn't happened, but we were ready, and we are still ready if it does.

A blind reliance on insufficient modeling has led some politicians to institute disastrous lockdowns that have not only jeopardized their people's health and welfare but also created conditions for a financial catastrophe that will cause untold burdens and costs on their people for generations.

While many can work remotely from their laptops indefinitely, a key takeaway from COVID is that America's essential workers—the farmers, the ranchers, truckers, plumbers, grocers, healthcare workers, the builders, and producers in this country—are more critical than ever. The fundamentals of life haven't changed. People still need basic necessities to survive, grocery stores need to stay stocked, lights need to stay on, and doctors need to keep seeing patients.

To the builders, the producers, and the essential workers scattered throughout the country: if you've seen how South Dakota has managed this pandemic and you like what you've seen, come to South Dakota. To those professionals who will be working from home permanently, if you value our way of life, where people love freedom, smaller communities, and lots of wide-open spaces, I want you to think about doing your work from a new home in South Dakota.

To business owners in other states who are frustrated that your business was forced to close, South Dakota has the friendliest tax and regulatory system in the nation. We didn't order businesses to close; we trusted them to innovate and to continue serving their customers, and we'd love for you to do your business here as well. South Dakota truly is open for business.

And to all those who've lost loved ones, my heart breaks for you.

Our new normal may be very different from the past, but don't ever forget this one fundamental truth: the windshield is so much bigger than the rearview mirror for a reason. In South Dakota, we always confront adversity, and we emerge into even greater prosperity. The future, our future, is bright. Hope is in front of us; we will come out stronger than ever before.

And to those concerned about what the future might hold for you if you stay where you are right now, come to South Dakota. The air is fresh, the people are free, and the possibilities are endless.

ALWAYS CHECK REFERENCES

Checking references applies to babysitters, job applicants, and those appointed to crisis-management positions. Let's remember this, because the next crisis is always around the corner.

Sadly, we've learned that many—perhaps most—in government will use fear to control us. And fear isn't the only tool of control. For example, I talk with people every day who say, "Yeah, we know TikTok's bad, but it's so funny. Did you see this video?" Social media is changing our culture, one mind at a time, and not because of some accident in a Chinese lab. It's intentional.

In early 2020, TikTok broke the record for most app downloads in a single three-month period. The Chinese developers knew what they were doing and chose their moment carefully. They waited until people were locked in their homes, and then they offered a "solution" in the form of a video app with the bonus of spyware.[7]

Seriously, Kristi, why are you so worked up about TikTok? What's the harm?

There's no harm—at least no *apparent* harm—until the next crisis. That's when the brainwashing is exposed.

Think about how many decades it took for the lie that the Holocaust never happened to proliferate. Sure, there were a few who tried to push that narrative from the 1940s, but it has taken decades for that denial to gain traction.

Just look at all the pro-Hamas and anti-Israel sentiment and the public demonstrations we've seen since Israel was attached on October 7, 2023. Did you see that coming?

How quickly people have become convinced that Hamas did not act inappropriately—and even deny video evidence of unspeakable Hamas's atrocities. (I've seen video footage from the attacks, and the brutality is inhuman.)

The world is allowing technology to be used by evil entities to push lies and rewrite history. And when we become detached from our history, we become detached from reality. This is dangerous to our freedom and our future. And I am alarmed that so many Americans—including our leaders—are not even willing to be inconvenienced to stop it. They'd rather be entertained than educated.

Perhaps that is because this generation has never experienced true hardship, and we may have to go through something truly terrible before we wake up to reality. My prayer is that I'm wrong, that we're wiser than this. And I pray there will be brave souls who will speak the truth and sound the alarm when our freedoms are under attack. *(And I'm not talking about fire alarms, Representative Jamaal Bowman.)*

THE LOYALTY LESSON

The real lesson from COVID is not about distrust; it's about *loyalty.* Hear me out.

Sure, we didn't have the luxury of time when it came to who to appoint and what to do. However, I believe we would have made much better choices if we were clear about where our loyalties were. And I'm not talking about allegiance to a political party.

You can be loyal and ask tough questions. In fact, I believe that's crucial.

If you're in a leadership position and expect loyalty from those around you, then be loyal to them. And make sure new team members have proven their devotion to the same values and ideals you hold.

When you're faced with impossible, no-win decisions, will you stay loyal to our Constitution? Our American principles? Your faith in God? To the people who you serve? To your family and true friends?

Loyalty means nothing when everything's smooth sailing. Following through on our core convictions in the face of horrific situations is where our true loyalties are revealed.

STEP FORWARD

What, and who, are you loyal to? As you step forward to help our nation move forward, your values and convictions will be tested.

The next flu strain could be brewing somewhere. Unthinkable tragedy might unfold in your state. Government leaders could, and probably will, try to limit your freedom of speech or right to assemble. A leader's decisions in the toughest moments are the most telling. Do you trust your leaders to make the right decisions?

Are you clear-minded about what you hold dear and who you hold dear?

Be ready. Be a leader.

WILL THE WORLD AWAKEN?

America must play its role in ushering in a new era of peace.

—President Barack Obama's inaugural address, 2009[1]

*I did not come here to guide lambs. I came
here to awaken lions.*

—Javier Milei, president-elect of Argentina in 2023[2]

I'll never forget waking up in Afghanistan after a twenty-hour trip, the last leg of which consisted of being strapped into a hard canvas seat inside a C-130 Hercules aircraft. They rolled us into Herat in the dark, around two that morning, and I tried to catch a few hours' sleep. At five a.m. I got up and asked one of the military liaisons if there was a treadmill I could use anywhere in the facility to burn off some steam.

The young military aide handed me a bottle of water and brought me to a lone 1980s-era treadmill that was situated next to a small window. As my eyes adjusted to the sunrise, I couldn't quite comprehend the view. There were multiple walls and fences topped with razor wire, and towers with machine gunners. Beyond the fortifications there was a dirt road, and beyond that—only desert and barren mountains. After a few minutes on the squeaky treadmill, I spotted a dozen kids playing soccer across the road.

They had no shoes, and their playground was one of the most dangerous places on earth at the time.

Where in the world am I? And how did I get here?

The contrasts were impossible to reconcile. There I was, a farmer from South Dakota, now an American congress-woman, surrounded by the finest fighting force in the world, stretching my legs on this rickety treadmill after a long trip. And it happened to be the week of Mother's Day, 2013. Outside the base, I watched as people were living their lives in what seemed like an alternate universe—an extremely dangerous one. Yet to them, it was normal. My kids were little at the time—the same age as most of the kids playing across the road.

As we traveled within the country, we were required to wear full body armor regardless of where we went. Marines surrounded each member of our delegation and instructed us to keep our heads down as we ran to vehicles and in and out of Blackhawk helicopters. Aboard the choppers, soldiers leaned out through open doors, looking for threats like rocket-propelled grenades. The tension was unrelenting; I don't know how they handled the pressure. And they did it for months at a time, on multiple deployments. Every time I returned from one of these visits I carried even more appreciation for the dedicated men and women of our military.

I always ask myself what it would be like to grow up in those war-torn countries. You don't get to be a policymaker and be devoid of human feelings. As governor, I am the commander in chief of our National Guard. We were the first state to send these troops to help at the southern border, and they have volunteered to be in harm's way all over the globe. You can't make good decisions if you don't have empathy and compassion for the people you're responsible for.

No one becomes an expert on another country, region, or culture with one visit, but one visit can be extremely informative. It can serve as a humble reminder of how little we know about the world. Every trip and every conversation with locals broaden your perspective. And for me, it also reinforces my belief in—and commitment to—American values.

WORLD FREEDOM

In November 2023 I was honored to speak at the Worldwide Freedom Initiative conference in Paris, along with Nigel Farage and other conservative voices from the United States and Europe.[3] My message centered around how we try to live out our freedom and conservative principles, reminding the audience that there's a lot more to the United States than New York City and Washington, DC.

While in Paris, I was slated to meet with French president Emmanuel Macron. However, the day before we were to meet he made what I considered a very pro-Hamas and anti-Israel comment to the press. So, I decided to cancel. There is no place for pro-Hamas rhetoric. Let me be clear, in case you didn't know this already: I support Israel's right to defend herself 100 percent.

What stood out to me was how closely Europeans were watching our nation—the good and the bad—and how hungry they were for the return of American leadership. I was also surprised at how many people knew about the successes we've had in South Dakota, especially during and after COVID. Standing up for freedom and asking commonsense questions resonates with citizens around the globe. When you talk with world leaders, you also realize what America really means to the world. Our presidential elections are a big deal to people in other nations because that "leader of the free world" title is real. What we do, and who we elect, matters more to other countries than most people would admit.

The lack of humanity and wisdom from the Biden administration's policies at our southern border is appalling. These actions and, more accurately, inactions qualify as neglect and abuse. Meanwhile Biden has cowered before Russia, while sending billions to Ukraine to pay for pensions for their government workers, with no accountability to the American taxpayer. What's even crazier is that we are borrowing the money from China to send to Ukraine.

In the long run, Biden's policies stifle true freedom. It's clear to me that they have no compass and therefore no leadership on the world stage. As a result, millions are suffering, and America is a laughingstock around the globe.

Don't even get me started about how the Biden administration treated our soldiers who refused to be injected with the COVID vaccine. Thousands of dedicated men and women were needlessly discharged from our military.[4] The Biden regime celebrates cross-dressing and diversity, equity, and inclusion in our armed forces but punishes soldiers who simply want to control their own medical choices.

I miss Ronald Reagan. Reagan understood "Peace through strength." And after the turbulent 1960s and 1970s, he made it cool to love America again. He increased funding for our military, ensured our fighting forces had the resources they needed to be successful, and cut taxes at the same time. Leaders lead. In 2024, we have the opportunity to send someone to the White House who has the same "America First" vision.

A GLOBAL VIEW

While in Congress, I served on the House Armed Services Committee and traveled often: Israel, Jordan, United Arab Emirates, Saudi Arabia, Afghanistan, China, Norway, Greece, Italy, and Egypt. But visiting South Korea and the demilitarized zone on the border with North Korea was particularly striking.

I can still remember the South Korean soldiers lined up along their country's border, facing the north. The North Korean soldiers were mere yards away. Between these two enemies stood American troops. Americans. Keeping peace.

The North Korean soldiers tried to antagonize our warriors, trying to spit on them, shouting at them, and trying to break their composure. Yet, our warriors stood strong. If ever there was an example of the role America plays in the world, it was there—in the flesh. Peace through strength.

CHINA

After a meeting with the president of South Korea, we went to China, where we held meetings with President Xi Jinping and members of his cabinet. Being in that communist dictatorship was another alternate universe. We were instructed that due to the intense spying operation the Chinese conduct, we couldn't take any of our electronics. Moreover, our security told us to be cautious about anything left behind in the hotel for fear of the rooms being ransacked. And they were. It was clear every time we returned to our hotel rooms that someone had rifled through our clothing and belongings. There were cameras on almost every street; the Chinese were watching and listening to our every move.

I couldn't imagine being a citizen of that country, living under such surveillance and scrutiny. That's why it matters when our government tries to impose communist-style surveillance on us, and why we must keep a close eye on our relationship with China.

When you think of South Dakota, you might think about rolling fields of corn and soybeans and hills full of cattle. You might think of the gorgeous Black Hills or Mount Rushmore—and if you can't picture them right now in your mind, then you need to come visit.

I am proud that South Dakota is a beacon of freedom. And in the last three years, we've been setting an example by drawing the blueprint for a state-led response to the Chinese Communist Party. We were the first state in America to propose blocking members of the Chinese Communist Party (CCP) from buying South Dakota agricultural land. As one of many examples, in 2015, CCP billionaire Chen Tianqiao purchased 200,000 acres of land in Oregon.[5] We don't want nations that hate us, and that work against us, to be part of our way of life.

Remember when a Chinese spy balloon spent days hovering over the American homeland. What did President Biden do? He lied and tried to change the subject. He attended a Democratic National Committee rally. He did nothing to stop the spy aircraft until it had already crossed our nation from west to east, sending critical data about our most valuable assets back to China. I happen to know that our armed forces had the ability to shoot down the balloon, but they were told not to. I put this in the category of President Biden not abiding by his oath to protect our nation from all enemies both foreign and domestic.

With Biden so weak on China, governors have to step up and take the lead. *More Freedom, Less China.* The Chinese military has increased in strength at an astounding pace. The CCP has manipulated China's currency for years. They've stolen American intellectual property while cheating on trade, and the globalist elites from both parties continue to allow it.

COVID wasn't the only thing that China exported. In the first quarter of 2020, TikTok broke the record for most downloads, and it still ranks among the most downloaded apps in the world. South Dakota put a stop to it—prohibiting state employees, agencies, and contractors from downloading or using the TikTok app or visiting the website on state-owned or state-leased devices. Months later, nearly thirty states have taken action against TikTok, and because of what we are doing in the states, Congress finally stepped up and banned it for US government devices.

I also signed a bill banning state and local governments from conducting business with six evil foreign governments, including China. The bill bans state and local governments from doing business with certain telecommunications companies associated with these governments. And it also blocks state contracts with companies owned, influenced, or affiliated with these countries. And it doesn't stop at China—this order also bans state business with Iran, North Korea, Russia, Cuba, and Venezuela.

Since my time in Congress, I've been sounding the alarm about what the Chinese Communist Party is doing *inside* the United States. They've been buying up our chemical and fertilizer companies and purchasing food processing companies.

In fact, they own the largest pork production facility in my state. Today, they're trying to buy up our land. Why? Because those who control food and energy supplies control the world. (Just look at how Russia has leveraged their energy resources to blackmail Europe.)

Between 2010 and 2020, the CCP's holdings of US agricultural land increased by 5,300 percent. They now own more than 350,000 acres of US agricultural land valued at almost $2 billion. That land could be farmed by about eight hundred American family farms. It's no coincidence that some of these parcels are close to military installations.

South Dakota has one of the premier military installations in America. It is the future home of the next generation of B-21 bombers, joining the mighty B-1s. (These B-1 bombers conducted several operations in the Middle East that made the news in early 2024.) Our pilots sat in those bombers for over thirty hours. Their seats in those decades-old aircraft are little and hard! I tried to climb into one of those bomber seats a few years ago and was worried they would have to pry me out. It's incredible what these crews endure to protect us. We also host MQ-9 Reaper drones. These assets need to be protected against all foreign surveillance and interference from adversaries.

The Chinese Communist Party is a clear and present danger to America. Why aren't our leaders in Washington treating them as such? Maybe they've never been to China or looked into the abyss of North Korea. Claiming ignorance doesn't work anymore.

MAKE EARTH GREAT AGAIN?

As horrifying and heartbreaking as China's rise is, I'm encouraged by commonsense conservatives making their case to citizens and winning elections all over the world. These leaders are untested in their new roles, but I'm encouraged by the results.

New Zealand's Christopher Luxon became prime minister in October 2023. I quoted his misguided, COVID-obsessed predecessor, Jacinda Ardern, in chapter 1. There have also been encouraging victories in the Netherlands, Argentina, Switzerland, and Italy. Last year in Hungary, Viktor Orbán won a fourth term.

In early 2024, Taiwan's anti-China party won a historic third term. But within minutes, President Biden made it clear that he bowed to Xi in a statement to reporters: "We do not support independence."[6] God help us, and God help the Taiwanese people.

In late 2023, farmers in France rose up in protest over growing regulations and sprayed manure on government buildings. I'm familiar with both manure and government buildings, and the pairing seems to be a poetic statement. Talking about fighting fire with fire. In January 2024, German farmers also joined together for massive protests against their government's overreach.

We will defend God, country, and family.
Those things that disgust people so much.
We will do it to defend our freedom.
—Giorgia Meloni [7]

AWAKENING IN ITALY
In early 2022 I had the opportunity to meet with Italy's Giorgia Meloni when we both spoke at the Conservative Political Action Committee conference. I was surprised and humbled

by her request for a meeting. Honestly, I wondered how she even knew who I was.

As I walked in the conference room for our meeting, she immediately rose from her chair and ran over to introduce herself. It was like we'd known each other for years. "I've been waiting so long to meet you. And I've heard so many wonderful things," she exclaimed. It was inspiring to listen to her story as a woman politician and answer her questions about leading as a strong woman. (People around the world really are looking to our nation for inspiration and freedom.)

The meeting was fantastic. She asked several insightful questions about fiscal discipline, conservative policies, running for office, and effective communication with the public. I instantly knew she would be a great leader. Of course, she went on to win her country's election for prime minister later that year.

Without betraying the moment, I'll say we had a very human conversation about being decisive and the double standards sometimes applied to women in leadership. We also discussed budgets and economics. It also struck me that there may not have been many women with similar personalities around her. Of course, we discussed COVID, and her campaign for national office.

Giorgia and I talked candidly about being ostracized for our beliefs and attacks from political enemies. I reassured her that we all face those challenges. "Other than the fact that these people want to destroy our very existence, what's the downside?" I joked.

In late 2023, she made it clear to China that Italy would have no part in their covert belt and road initiatives.[8] *Salute, Giorgia!*

BAD DAY TO BE A GOAT

Back in the USA, harvest season is like the Super Bowl of farming. It's the culmination of months of hard work where, if everything goes right, you'll celebrate a job well done. Harvest requires long hours of physical labor in harsh weather struggling to get the crop in before Mother Nature shuts you down. Prime harvest season also happens to be prime hunting season. Running a hunting lodge during harvest is insane. Balancing both at full throttle is enough to break a family.

One particularly stressful year, one of the last groups of guests at our lodge was from Georgia. They were longtime friends who made the annual trip to our property many years in a row. I'd be their guide all week, and we had strategically pushed birds to an eighty-acre tract of habitat. I wanted these guys to have an amazing amount of success on their final morning of hunting before they went back home. It promised to be a fantastic day of bagging pheasant—our state bird.

I decided to take a few experienced dogs out that morning, and one young dog named Cricket. We hunted with pointers and retrievers, which usually made a good combination in the types of habitat we worked. Cricket was a wirehair pointer, about fourteen months old, and she had come to us from a home that struggled with her aggressive personality. I was sure she'd learn a lot going out with our older dogs that day.

I was wrong.

Within an hour of walking the first field, Cricket had blown past the group, gotten too far ahead, and flushed up birds out of range. She was out of her mind with excitement, chasing all those birds and having the time of her life. The only problem was there were no hunters nearby to shoot the birds she scared up.

I called her back to no avail. I hit her electronic collar to give her a quick tone to remind her to listen. I then hit the button to give her a warning vibration that told her to come back to me. No response. We all watched helplessly as dozens and dozens of pheasants exploded from the grass and flew out of sight. The hunt was ruined. I was livid.

After the hunters left for the airport, I started to load kennels in my pickup in order to haul all the dogs back to the ranch. As I loaded the dogs and supplies, I realized I was one kennel short. No matter. I would just let Cricket ride loose in the back end of the truck on the way home. If she was dumb enough to jump out, then good riddance. After what she had pulled that day, I didn't care.

Some neighbors who recently purchased a puppy from us asked me to stop and check on their pup on the way home. As I pulled into their driveway, I saw the couple standing in the yard waiting for me—the mother carried a toddler on her hip. I brought the truck to a stop, got out, and started to play with the puppy and make small talk. Suddenly, out of the corner of my eye, I caught a glimpse of Cricket launching herself out of the back end of the pickup truck and racing across the yard. As I swung around to see what she was after, my stomach dropped.

Chickens.

I immediately took off sprinting across the yard, yelling, "Come! Cricket, come!"

Once again, she didn't even flinch.

I could hear the mother behind me yelling "My chickens! No, not my chickens!" as she sobbed and ran after me, bouncing the baby under her arm. All three of us chased Cricket around in circles, flailing after her while she systematically grabbed one chicken at a time, crunching it to death with one bite, then dropping it to attack another. She was a trained assassin.

Eventually I got my hand on her collar, and she whipped around to bite me. Shocked, I dragged her back to my pickup and threw her inside the cab. I took my checkbook out, grabbed a pen, slammed the door, and faced the music.

There were bloodied bodies and feathers everywhere.

"How much do I owe you for the chickens?" I ask flatly.

The mother had tears running down her cheeks. Her husband kept saying over and over how much they loved those chickens, how they were a part of their family, and that they were irreplaceable. I kept apologizing, wrote them a check for the price they asked, and helped them dispose of the carcasses littering the scene of the crime.

When I got back into my truck, Cricket was sitting in the passenger seat, looking like she just won the lottery. The picture of pure joy.

I hated that dog.

As I drove home, I realized that I had no choice. Cricket was untrainable and, after trying to bite me, dangerous to anyone she came in contact with. A dog who bites is dangerous and unpredictable (are you listening, Joe Biden?)—especially if you are running a business where people interact with your dogs. Besides that, she was less than worthless to us as a hunting dog.

At that moment, I realized I had to put her down.

As I pulled into the driveway, I decided that I had to deal with this problem myself. This was my dog and my responsibility, and I would not ask someone else to clean up my mess. I stopped the truck in the middle of the yard, got my gun, grabbed Cricket's leash and led her out into the pasture and down into the gravel pit.

It was not a pleasant job—but it had to be done. And after it was over, I realized another unpleasant job needed to be done. Walking back up to the yard, I spotted our billy goat.

This goat had been a problem for years. He was nasty and mean, as most male goats are that are left uncastrated. Male goats urinate on their own heads and beards while in rut, hoping to attract females with their putrid smell. It's the most disgusting, musky, rancid smell you can imagine.

Not only was this goat constantly covered in his own muck, but he also loved to chase the kids. He would knock them down and butt them. The wretched smell was impossible to get out of their clothes, and we had to burn too many shirts and jeans. Needless to say, the children were terrified of this animal. I would often find them on a fence or piece of equipment, held hostage by the demon goat. So, while taking care of unpleasant business, I decided now was as good a time as any to dispose of this problem, too.

I went down to the corral, caught the goat, and dragged him out to the gravel pit. I tied him to a post. But when I went to shoot him, he jumped at the last second. My shot was off and I needed one more shell to finish the job. Problem was, I didn't have one. Not wanting him to suffer, I hustled back across the pasture to the pickup, grabbed another shell, hurried back to the gravel pit, and put him down.

As I came back up out of the gravel pit and crossed the pasture, I looked up to the yard, where our new home was under construction. I had an audience. The construction crew had been sitting outside in a group taking their afternoon coffee break, watching the entire drama—with looks of shocked amazement on their faces.

When they saw me heading their way, they put their cups down, got up, and went back to work—in a real hurry.

Right about then, the school bus pulled into the yard and the kids jumped off, excited to see all the hunting dogs home. As we let the dogs out of their kennels, Kennedy looked around confused and asked, "Hey, where's Cricket?"

Later that evening, my uncle, who was the general contractor building our house, called me and said, "What got into you today?"

"Nothing," I responded. "Why?"

"Well, the guys said you came barreling into the yard with your truck, slammed the door, and took a gun and a dog over the hill, out of sight. They heard one shot and you came back without the dog. Then you grabbed the goat and headed back up over the hill. They heard another shot, you came back, slammed the pickup door, went back. Then they heard another shot and then you came back without the goat. They said they hurried back to work before you decided they were next!"

I guess, if I were a better politician I wouldn't tell the story here. But I never ask anyone else to do my job for me, even if it's difficult, messy, and ugly. I've made plenty of mistakes, but ignoring problems has never been one of them.

Being a leader isn't always fun, and leadership isn't limited to speeches and internal meetings. It's often messy, ugly, and matter-of-fact, dealing with a problem that no one wants to deal with. The world is full of talkers and "avoiders." We need doers.

THE NOEM DOCTRINE

When I see the decline of our nation on the world stage over decades, but also since 2021, I believe we need guiding principles to move forward. Here are my thoughts.

America First but not America alone. This applies to trade and international conflict. We can't lead the world if we abandon our own interests. And if other nations abandon us and our values, we'll remember.

Peace through strength. Stay out of local and tribal conflicts, and never appease. Draw bright red lines and respond fiercely and instantly when they are crossed. Our enemies should fear us, and we must give them reason to.

Fight to win. Fully fund our military. Use every diplomatic and strategic tool. Sanctions and freezing bank accounts of bad actors can be effective, but the actual results need to be measured. Sanctions can actually backfire, and we may be watching this consequence with the Russian ruble and China's move away from the US dollar. Do I even need to state that we must *never* send money to our enemies? Every path to victory should be on the table, and every war should be won as quickly as possible.

Our military is a force for both kindness and killing. Our brave soldiers represent us in all kinds of situations. But when it comes to defending good guys and eliminating bad ones, we're unapologetically lethal. And our armed forces are not a lab for social and gender experiments.

Immigration is a national security issue. We need to know who is coming here and why. If there's not a good reason (and we decide what a good reason is), they go back. If they stay, we help them assimilate. If they entered illegally, they don't get to stay. Cutting the line doesn't work.

Our intelligence community should be spying on China, not on law-abiding citizens. Clear enough?

In 2015 and 2016 many skeptics and pundits predicted a Trump presidency would get America into World War III. "He has no foreign policy experience!" the experts shrieked. Wars didn't happen—quite the opposite—and a peace accord in the Middle East was moving forward. Now, since 2021, the "adults" are in charge and hell has broken loose across the globe.

ISRAEL

I suppose Israeli prime minister Benjamin Netanyahu has a lot in common with Donald Trump in terms of balancing a strong vision with respect for other voices.

The first visit I had with Netanyahu in Jerusalem was amazing. I was a no-name freshman member of Congress, sitting at a table with many other leaders. Prime Minister Netanyahu looked at me and asked, "What would you like to add today, Congresswoman Noem? How are things in South Dakota?" He knew my name, and he knew where I was from.

He'd done his homework. Of course, I did have some things to say and questions to ask. But what astonished me was that he went out of his way to hear my insights. In subsequent meetings over the years, he always remembered our previous conversations.

I appreciate the fact that he influences by telling stories—sadly, mostly tragic ones about needless violence against his citizens. But he makes compelling cases for his vision. Despite political turmoil, he holds steady. He's a fighter.

The two most memorable foreign leaders I've met are Netanyahu and Boris Johnson of the United Kingdom. I think it's safe to say these two were at opposite ends of the spectrum in some funny ways.

CASH COW

Years ago, I had the honor of spending a week in Kenya, on a congressional trip with World Vision. We were there to see refugee camps, meet with tribal leaders, and have a firsthand look at what USAID was doing in the region.

As you might know or imagine, there's a lot to be surprised and saddened by in situations like this. We met precious people in camps who had lived there for decades, surviving on daily handouts. Some were born there and know nothing else.

Outside the barbed wire fences of the camp we saw families on the brink of starvation. But they refused to resign themselves to the life of dependency inside that fence. We met a withered but resilient grandma who was raising her grandchildren, because all her children had died from AIDS. She and her grandkids would go to the jungle and harvest fruit, then sell it to local villages.

The money they earned allowed them to buy food. She was so proud of her business and the difference it made for her family. But when she showed me her cow, she beamed. Her dream was to save enough money to buy a second cow, not just to have more milk for her family, but to sell milk to others, meet a need in her community, and earn more for her family.

As our group stood around and heard her story through the translators, I was overwhelmed. It would take one or two years to save the money necessary to purchase that second cow. Looking at the translator, I asked, "How much is a cow?!" He seemed confused, and I was stirred up. "I'm a rancher. How much does a cow cost? Can I buy her one right now?"

Discussion buzzed among the translators and handlers. I tried to be patient and let them have their discussion, but this situation seemed like an easy fix. I had seen cows a few miles down the road. *Why not just go down there and buy her one—today?*

Finally, after what seemed like a United Nations deliberation, they told me a cow would cost about forty US dollars, and added, "But we can't do that right now. It's too complicated. Let us find out." After I staged a one-woman protest, they assured me they would get back to me, tell me how much money to send, and email a photo of the new cow when it arrived at the grandmother's house. Grandma was ecstatic at the news that I was going to help her get a cow. I was annoyed by the delay, but we went on with our itinerary.

Back in DC, my staff and I called the nonprofit almost every week, asking about the blessed cow.

It was almost nine months later when she finally got her cow, and I finally got the bill. It was $840.92.

Another perfect example of government dysfunction. I bet you forty bucks there was a cow down the road for sale, and we could have taken care of business in about ten minutes. They did finally send me a picture of her hugging that cow. Also pictured were the team of "cow consultants" who helped make it all possible.

Next time you hear about a billion dollars going to Ukraine or anywhere in the world, I hope you'll remember this cash cow story. It doesn't have to be that way.

STEP FORWARD

Before taking these many trips outside the United States, I didn't fully comprehend the ripple effect of every decision our leaders make. Travel and conversations have made me more compassionate, more humble, and much bolder. Everyone's an expert on world affairs until they step off that helicopter.

That's an old Chinese proverb: "I hear and I forget; I see and I remember; I do and I understand."

When it comes to this beautiful and brutal world, get out there and see what it's like for others. Do some good.

And let's elect leaders with some understanding.

SEVEN

THE WOLF PACK

And I said, "Well, gosh, can't we find some women that
are also qualified?" I went to a number of women's
groups and said, "Can you help us find folks?" and they
brought us whole binders full of women.

—PRESIDENTIAL CANDIDATE MITT ROMNEY, OCTOBER 2012[1]

*As women achieve power, the barriers will fall. As
society sees what women can do, as women see what
women can do, there will be more women out there
doing things, and we'll all be better off for it.*

—JUSTICE SANDRA DAY O'CONNOR[2]

July 3, 2020, was a monumental day in South Dakota history and our national history. After years of bureaucratic wrangling against the US Department of the Interior, the fireworks celebration at Mount Rushmore was back on! And the president of the United States would be in attendance to celebrate our country's birthday with us.

It's impossible to describe the huge amount of preparation that went into making that day successful and safe. Our staff worked around the clock to make sure everything was perfect, and a surprising cast of volunteers rolled into action. When I had the privilege of stepping up to the microphone to begin the program, I shared what I believed was an important message for our nation. Here are just a few of those words, which apply to us today: "We must all renew our commitment to a country where any person, regardless of his or her standing at birth, can make anything of themselves. Like me. I was just a farm kid. Now I am the first female governor of South Dakota. Let us all, like our founding fathers, pledge our own lives, our fortunes, our sacred honor, to the cause of liberty and self-government. So that we may continue to have the freedom to follow our conscience, to build our lives, and to live in peace."

The military flyovers, the speeches—including one from President Trump—the fireworks, and the complex logistics went perfectly. Special thanks are due to thousands of dedicated members of law enforcement and our National Guard who made sure we all enjoyed a peaceful celebration.

Because this gathering occurred during the first few months of the pandemic—and after "two weeks to flatten the curve" turned into many months of shutdowns—people from all over the country were watching the celebration. The media was intent on labeling it a "super-spreader" event. The fact is, we never identified a single COVID case caused by that incredible celebration.

Images of fireworks over Mount Rushmore always make the national news, so later that evening I asked our team for an update on what was trending on social media. As I entered the Blackhawk helicopter with President Trump on the way back to Air Force One, staffers informed me that the celebration was getting a lot of attention on social media—but not the kind I expected. "Kristi Noem's arms" was trending on Twitter.

Really? I thought, shaking my head. *After an incredible celebration and all the heartfelt words spoken, the talk on social media and in the press was about a sleeveless dress?*

As I flew that night to Washington, DC, on Air Force One (my first time on that impressive mobile office), some of the president's staff also said, "They're tweeting about your arms." By that time, I decided to just laugh about it. Little did I know that just a few months later, an even bigger "faux pas" would erupt.

In February 2021, I spoke at the Conservative Political Action Committee conference, again delivering what I believed was a crucial message for our time. The speech was well received. But for some liberal pundits and social media critics, the big story was that I had the gall to wear the same red dress I wore at Mount Rushmore.

Disappointingly, the same pundits who are quick to call out anything resembling sexism from conservatives were fixated on a wardrobe choice.

Even in 2024, one of the strange things about being a woman is the constant attention from the media on what we wear. Yes, I do believe that how we present ourselves matters. But there's still a different standard for women (#Fetterman) perpetuated by the shallow media. Regardless, I'll still wear what's appropriate for the occasion and trust that most people are listening to what I say.

Let's not be fooled by the media. Are they really concerned about hair, clothing, and makeup? No, they're laser-focused on diminishing our message. It's an intentional distraction and, sadly, very effective in terms of clickbait headlines and social media impressions.

Ignore their shallowness, and keep moving the conversation forward.

DIFFERENTIATION, NOT LIMITATION

I love the fact that, when I was growing up, my mom, my dad, and folks at the ranch didn't expect less of me because I was a girl. My parents acknowledged the wonderful differences between men and women, but treated us the same and gave us equal opportunity. Bryon and I always did the same with our kids, and now our grandkids. We celebrate the differences but *remove all limitations.*

What's astonishing is that the liberal "feminists" who helped fight for Title Nine and equality for women in sports are undermining those gains today. In trying to give a tiny percentage of the population a misguided affirmation about gender, they're killing opportunities for millions of girls— and I won't stand for it.

Joe Biden's America doesn't even recognize the basic differences between biological males and females—nor are they willing to define what a woman is. In South Dakota I introduced and signed into law the strongest bill in the nation to protect girls' and defend fairness for women. Here's the backstory.

When the state legislature passed a very flawed bill regarding biological men participating in women's sports and put it on my desk in 2021, we quickly realized there were some real dangers if I signed it into law. It opened the state and public school districts to expensive litigation exposure because of poor verbiage and terminology. It also would have allowed students suffering from asthma or breathing problems or need-ing cortisone shots to be kicked off of sports teams because of their use of steroids to control their physical ailments.

This bill would have been immediately mired in lawsuits, and we would have lost, setting the movement to protect girls' sports back. Some political strategists said I should have just signed it into law in order to avoid any criticism and take a victory lap. They said I could probably improve the flaws during the next legislative session. I told them quite clearly that I was not in the business of signing flawed legislation into law. We do it right the first time, even when it's difficult or unpopular.

As a governor, I don't get the "luxury" of signing bad bills. My responsibility is to sign the best constitutional bills into law and defend them in court if necessary. And sadly, it's increasingly necessary.

Many people would say I lost the messaging war on that bill. And in hindsight, I would have communicated more clearly and forcefully. There was much confusion, and my political enemies changed the facts to fit their narrative and tried to make themselves look more conservative. But the facts remain. I have always supported legislation that would ensure males could not participate in female sports in our schools and universities. But I was determined to pursue a legislative pathway that allowed us to win the argument not only in the court of public opinion but also in our judicial sys-tem, so we could keep policies in place.

As governor, I have the ability to make modifications, or "style and form" changes, to legislation, and that's exactly what I did. After I modified the bill so only girls would play girls sports, I sent it back to the legislature.

And they rejected the bill. Several men in the legislature took a "tuck" and run approach to the clear language.

I immediately signed two executive orders to protect girls and their sports, but few paid attention. As a former athlete and a mom to former high school and college athletes, I was shocked that some conservative commentators were so outraged by my rejection of the original bill. Had they done their homework, instead of going for sensational headlines and clicks, I'm confident they would have been cheering what we accomplished in South Dakota. And too few remember who I fought for and won the case to keep males out of female rodeo events—in 2018!

OUR WOLF PACK

A few years ago, I had the honor of working with a gifted young woman and accomplished athlete named Madison Sheahan. She actually moved to South Dakota to work and travel with me. She was passionate about leadership and rowed on *the* Ohio State University national championship team, so she was also highly competitive. As we were making small talk one day about women in leadership, she asked me, "Have you ever read a book called *Wolfpack*?"[3] I hadn't. "It's by World Cup soccer player Abby Wambach. You guys don't have much in common politically, but I think you'd really like it."

The next day she brought me the book, and I read it all in one sitting. Sure, there are many things Abby and I probably don't agree on, but I particularly loved one of the book's core leadership messages to girls and women, centered around the story of Little Red Riding Hood. Here are a few of my takeaways.

Generally speaking, little girls are told what they should be and what they shouldn't be. Boys can be rough and noisy and loud, and girls should be nice and proper and quiet. The opening chapter in the book references that even the fairy tales we tell our children are formative in the way they see themselves in the future and the lessons they learn on how to approach life. In the story of Little Red Riding Hood, the lesson is clear: *stay on the safe path that's clearly marked out for you—or there will be trouble!*

Yes, I'm all in for giving children boundaries and role models. I'm just not for limitations based on fear. And my whole life is about taking risks.

Abby shares in this first chapter that as she reflects on her life, her biggest opportunities for success came from times she ventured off the path, when she took a risk. She made a statement at the end of this chapter that hit me like a ton of bricks: "If I could go back and tell my younger self one thing, it would be this: 'Abby, you were never Little Red Riding Hood. You were always the Wolf.'"

Wow, that's how I had felt my whole life. Like I had a wolf inside me. I was aching to take risks and have great adventures, yet somehow every time I stepped out, people looked at me strangely or pointed out how different I was—as a girl. I was blessed to have a dad who didn't view me this way, but many others did, and it left an indelible impression on me from the time I was young. Those words in that book crystalized how I felt my whole life. And I loved it!

I have always been a wolf, but few had ever validated me. Even after Dad died, in the middle of intense shock and grief, something bold and strong rose up in me. I wanted to take over managing the ranch. I felt desperate to become the general manager of the operation, although I didn't dare voice it to my family. I mean, I'm the third oldest child, and my mom is still alive and well. Who am I to think I could run the business—and run it well? It was a strange desire to have, right? Well, that's exactly who I am.

Even though Abby and I have lived very different lives, we had some of the same experiences or feelings about what it was like to be a woman venturing off the established path and into the wild unknown.

Our culture and our politics are so messed up—and so engrained. Subconsciously we all have beliefs and assumptions that can limit us. That's why in the book you're holding and with those around me I want to help people realize that we can spur each other on and still embrace our individuality. And dammit, women need to have each other's backs. It's been decades of the good old boys running the world, and it's past time for women to ditch the infighting and show loyalty to female leaders and those who should be leading. In case you haven't noticed, I find it frustrating—no, *disgusting*—when insecure women compete with each other rather than help each other reach higher.

I've started several wolf packs with women and seen how strong the fairy tales have taken hold in our minds. Some stay stuck playing Little Red Riding Hood, trying to get along nicely and following the voices—internal and external—that remind them of their "place." I've encouraged women to run for leadership positions in our state legislature, offering my full support, only to have some of them tell me, "No, I'll wait, because the men have told me it's not quite my time."

I'm sorry, but that's bullshit. Even with my endorsement of their candidacy from my position as governor and my belief in their unique talents, some still hesitate and refuse to use their ability to the fullest. It grieves me to see them decline opportunities, because we all lose out.

But others hear the call of the wild (apologies for another book reference), follow their hearts, and jump into their adventure. They will make mistakes, just as I do. And they will be criticized. But they are in the arena, making a positive difference, and living a life of significance. Even if I don't totally agree with their politics, I say, "Go get 'em, girls!"

There's a wolf pack in my office right now (cue the sound of howling in the distance). It kind of happened by accident, but not really. Several phenomenal women run the governor's office, and they are absolutely brilliant and inspiring. They rose to higher positions by doing their jobs with excellence, offering solutions when others focused on problems, and keeping a balanced life and positive attitude. When we had leadership vacuums, they stepped up and offered to pick up duties that were not their responsibility, and they offered advice to me when others decided not to speak up. Not only that, in their private lives they are kicking butt—remodeling their houses; hunting big game with their spouses; raising incredible, caring children and often bringing them to the office; and attending our video meetings while giving their babies a bath. I can already see the ripple effect on the entire staff. It's inspirational.

Can you teach an old wolf new tricks? *Absolutely!* (Am I calling myself old? *No way!*) But I'm starting to believe that to turn our communities, states, and nation around, we need to find people who don't need to unlearn so much about politics—people who simply know how to get stuff done.

The concept of a wolf pack isn't as foreign to men; they've been gathering and encouraging each other to do great things for centuries. And in nature, real packs of wolves are led by an alpha couple—male and female.

Go find a wolf pack. Start one. Invite grandma—and your little girls. Women should have each other's backs and encourage each other to go far.

BEWARE THE LONE WOLF

One day in the summer of 2021, I was hauling a trailer full of horses on a long drive to get them new shoes. (That's my idea of shoe shopping, by the way.) My executive assistant called my cell phone and said, "We just got a call from Nikki Haley's office, and she'd like to schedule a phone call with you."

"Okay, I'll be driving for a couple hours. Just go ahead and give her my cell phone number," I replied, as I often do.

"Well, she doesn't want to do that. They are insisting on scheduling a call."

Okay, I thought. *That's weird.* "Just pick a time, then, and tell her to call me on my cell phone. I'll make sure I pick up."

About thirty minutes later my phone rang, and here's how I remember the conversation. "Hi, Governor Noem, this is Ambassador Haley's executive assistant. She is ready to speak to you now. I'll go ahead and put her on the call." I waited on hold until I heard the line connect. Basically, the conversation went like this.

"Hi, Governor, this is Ambassador Nikki Haley, and I just wanted to introduce myself and have a conversation. I just wanted to let you know that I follow you quite a bit. I have heard quite a bit about you, and you are doing a good job there in South Dakota. I was thinking that maybe you might like a mentor, and maybe I could be someone who could do that for you. Because you're a governor, you've gone through some challenging things that I did as well. I would be more than willing to be a mentor, because you've never been in this type of role before."

She went on to tell me about her life story, her résumé, and some of the challenges she faced in her legislature as governor and as ambassador to the United Nations reading daily talking points from the State Department. Once again, I recall, she offered to mentor me, as she was sure I was facing some decisions and situations I'd never seen before.

"I appreciate that offer. Thank you, and I will certainly let you know," I replied. "How do I get a hold of you?"

"You can reach out to my executive assistant."

"Okay. You can hang on to this number; it's my personal cell. Call me anytime," I said.

After what seemed to me a bit of an awkward pause, she added, "I . . . just . . . also want you to know one more thing . . . I've heard a lot of really good things about you. But I also want you to know that if I hear something bad . . . I will be sure to let you know."

There was a long pause.

"Um, well, thanks for that, Ambassador."

"Let me be clear," she added. "I've heard many good things about you. But when I do hear bad things, I will make sure that you know. I've enjoyed talking to you. We will visit soon. Goodbye." Click.

I took a few minutes to process the experience, and then dialed my executive assistant. "How did the call go?" she asked.

"I think I was just threatened by Nikki Haley?"

"What?!"

"Yeah, I'm pretty sure I was just threatened by Nikki Haley. It was clear that she wanted me to know that there was only room for one Republican woman in the spotlight. It was weird."

Unsurprisingly, I never received any calls or "mentoring" from her, but the message was clear. *I'm the alpha female here, and you should know your place.* I actually felt a little sad for her.

Besides whatever motivated her call, I suppose she didn't even realize that, unlike her, I was in Congress for eight years. In Washington, I held several leadership roles and served on several committees—including the Armed Services Committee, with numerous meetings with world leaders—while she was governor of South Carolina.

The day after January 6, 2021, I did have a brief conversation with Nikki at the RNC meeting. In my speech I talked about the importance of continuing to support Donald J. Trump, regardless of the fact that what unfolded on January 6 was undeniably ugly. She used the podium to criticize and distance herself from the former president.

"I think he's going to find himself further and further isolated," she declared. "I think he's lost any sort of political viability he was going to have. [. . .] He's not going to run for federal office again. [. . .] I don't think he's going to be in the picture. [. . .] I don't think he can. He's fallen so far."[4]

A few months later she told the *Wall Street Journal*, "He has the ability to get strong people elected, and he has the ability to move the ball, and I hope that he continues to do that. We need him in the Republican Party. I don't want us to go back to the days before Trump."[5] Then, in January 2024, referring to the primaries, she confessed, "The structure of it is really amazing. [. . .] Iowa starts it. You change personalities, you go into New Hampshire."[6]

That's the thing with Nikki Haley: you never know who she's going to be tomorrow. She's going to be whatever the polls or donors tell her to be. And that should be very scary to the American people. The people who know her the best, including some colleagues in her home state, seem to have the same concerns.

Maybe Nikki thinks she's a lone wolf. Or maybe it's about what Margaret Thatcher once said: "Being powerful is like being a lady. If you have to tell people you are, you aren't."[7]

HIGH CHAIRS

There's a funny difference between being in Congress and being a governor—and I've seen this across the country. When you're in Congress and attend an event, you get the requisite "pity applause" and most people call you by your first name. Governors are traditionally addressed as "Governor so-and-so," and people stand when you take the microphone. But it took me a while to catch on to this and form my own perspective.

Whenever I meet someone in South Dakota for the first time, I'm kind of shocked. *I thought I'd met everyone by now!* When I was a rancher, a business owner, and a mom at school meetings, I was always Kristi, and that was fine by me as a representative and as a new governor. But in an early staff meeting as governor one of my senior advisors noticed that even though I carried the new title, the press and attendees were still calling me by my first name and not standing when I entered a room like they did for the previous governor's events. This advisor announced to the entire staff, "From now on at events, I want a couple of you staffers sitting towards the front of the room. When the governor is introduced, stand up and start clapping, others will follow your example of this long-standing custom."

"No, no," I interrupted. "We don't have to do that."

"Governor!" she replied, shaking her finger at me. "Maybe it doesn't matter to *you*. But it matters to the next governor and the governor after that. You are not going to be the one that undermines the respect of the institution and of the office."

Class dismissed. Respect for the office was important to uphold, regardless of my informal style. By the way, that wise senior staffer was Beth, whom you met in chapter 3. As I reflected on her words of advice, I realized that I didn't want to be the governor who allowed respect for the office to diminish. And I knew the formalities were not about me; they were about the office, and that's a humbling perspective.

This conversation and a talk with a local historian also led me to move the governor's office from a tiny reception room to its historical location in the capitol, and relocate the original conference table from the local museum back to its place from the early days of statehood. Of course, the press and the haters twisted the move as a play to my ego. The truth is, besides the historical reasons, my team and I have a lot of meetings, and the former office was simply too small.

After we moved into the new office and were seated around the huge table, we noticed two things. First, our conversations felt weightier—like we had a fresh understanding of the honor of representing the people of our state. Second, those original chairs were gigantic! My feet couldn't touch the floor, and I'm five foot eight. Most of my staff faced the same challenge.

Once again, our resident historian informed us that the seating was intentionally crafted on this scale so when people sat down they'd realize that the job was bigger than they were, and that the seat would be there long after they were a distant memory. Every time I walk into the governor's office and sit in those chairs, I'm reminded that the office will be here for decades after I'm gone, and this job is way bigger than I am. I am simply honored to sit in the seat for a short period of time, all thanks to the people who trusted me enough to serve them.

Respect isn't something a leader demands. Respect is earned. And leaders must remember that it's the *title* they hold—temporarily—that deserves the honor.

WOMEN AND NEGOTIATIONS

When in Congress I worked with Illinois Democrat Jan Schakowsky on a bill to support the presence of women in international peace negotiations. The Women, Peace, and Security Act would, for the first time, establish women's participation as a permanent element of US foreign policy under congressional oversight. Because I served on the Armed Services Committee, had traveled quite a bit, and had been involved in several trade and peace negotiation discussions, I started digging into the statistics of what makes for successful negotiations.

I discovered that a peace negotiation was 35 percent more likely to last at least fifteen years when women were at the table. I'm sure there are several reasons for this, but one aspect stood out: whether a conflict is between countries or tribes, most men focus on the battles, and most of the women run the families, education, businesses, and become more involved in the day-to-day work of their communities.

The research made sense. For a negotiated peace agreement to endure, the long-term perspective of these women was crucial. Our bill required there to be at least one woman at the table in these discussions. I know, that might sound "feminist" and all about diversity, equity, and inclusion, but it's really about diversity of perspective. Men and women generally have different roles during war, and I happen to believe God made men and women different for a reason—we're designed to work together.

The bill finally passed, with quite a "diverse" group of lawmakers.[8]

STEP FORWARD

Whether you're a man or a woman, success and effective leadership are the results of taking risks. But what's crucial is the moment right before we make the final choice to step forward—or not.

Will we listen to the doubters around us, or believe the voices of those who have faith in us?

Can we overrule the doubt *inside*, and trust our heart?

Will we try to go it alone, or find a pack?

Can we cheer each other on, and give selflessly to help them succeed?

For much of my life, I felt like something was wrong with me—even broken. Whether it was natural sassiness, "talking back" to grown-ups as a little girl, or feeling pressure to apologize for being a good decision maker, it took me years to finally realize there wasn't anything wrong with being a strong, confident leader. I just needed wisdom and a heart for the people around me.

Ignore the naysayers, even if you've been one of them. And keep moving forward.

EIGHT

JUST BECAUSE YOU'RE PARANOID

It's not important what religion I believe in.
What's important is what America I believe in.

—Nancy Pelosi[1]

*Who is society? There is no such thing! There
are individual men and women, and there are
families, and no government can do anything
except through people.*

—Margaret Thatcher[2]

Growing up, we never talked politics in our family. My parents lived them.

My dad was a guy who got a brand-new pickup almost every year, with the options he liked. Remember bag phones? He was one of the very first in the area to have one. His truck was a big deal because it was his office.

I remember being out in the yard one day and watching Dad take a knife to his brand-new pickup, fresh from the dealership. He was cutting the seat belts out. "What are you doing?" I asked, wide-eyed.

"The government is trying to pass a law to say we're required to wear seat belts. No government is going to tell me I have to wear them," he said matter-of-factly. "So I'm taking them out." (This was a couple years before South Dakota enacted its own seat belt law.)

Even as a young woman, the message was clear: the government telling us what to do was not right. But there was an even deeper message in this example and a million others I witnessed from my parents: we don't just talk; we take action. We don't complain about things; we fix them. And we defend our freedoms. I learned the same lesson about faith—it's about living it.

I always try to remember to wear my seat belt, but still hold the same core conviction about Washington, DC, telling us how to live our lives.

FROM REVERSE TO FORWARD

We know that this country seems to be sliding backward and into a ditch, all at once. Time-tested truth and values are being attacked. Our society is becoming unhinged. And too many people in government seem to be cheering it on.

Because they have no real knowledge of history—and therefore no understanding of history—more and more people seem to have an outright disdain for our nation. I believe this shift is also rooted in a loss of appreciation for our traditional Judeo-Christian values.

Many people I speak with are discouraged—believing there's no hope and there's nothing that can be done to stop the downward slide. But that's just not true. We've lost ground because we haven't taken action in ways that work. Here's just one example of what the people of South Dakota accomplished, against all odds.

YOU HAVE TO STOP POT!

The life you've lived makes you into the person you are. In other words, personal history shapes personal convictions. I grew up in a family that didn't drink, didn't smoke, and didn't even play cards because it might lead to gambling. We were in church every time the doors were open, which was Sunday morning, Sunday night, and Wednesday night. We kids were involved in all the church youth activities.

When I became a mom, I also tried to live out our values and steer our children in the right direction, based on our faith and influenced by the way I was raised.

As someone entering the arena of public office, I was faced with the fact that not everyone shares the same faith or values or traditions as me—and I'm okay with that reality and respect people's honest convictions. The job I was elected to do, whether in the state legislature, in Congress, or as governor, is to uphold our state and federal constitutions.

Yes, my view on what's best for those I serve absolutely influences my policy positions, but I must work within the law to move issues forward or stop what I believe is harmful.

In 2020 the issue of legalizing marijuana was proposed in South Dakota. Based on what was happening in other states, it seemed that normalizing pot shops was inevitable. But as I traveled around the state, thousands of people came to me and pleaded, "Governor, you have to stop pot! You can't let it pass on the ballot."

I was, and still am, personally opposed to legalizing recreational pot. And that position was informed by many discussions while in the state legislature and Congress regarding the Substance Abuse and Mental Health Services Administration, and as governor in discussions with the Trump White House regarding drug policy.

When I spoke with those concerned about the possibility of legalization, I reminded them of the mechanism we had in place to address the question. "I'm with you," I'd say, "and the *whole state* gets to vote on it. I get one vote just like you."

WHY NOT?

Every study I reviewed showed that a significant percentage of people who did drugs ended up experiencing harmful consequences, including regular pot users relying more on government programs. I'd also say the vast majority of women and men in our prison system had addiction or drug use issues that were a factor in their criminal activity.

We also saw alarming research that showed that regular marijuana use could significantly affect brain development in those age twenty-six and younger, and it was a contributing factor in later mental health issues. I couldn't ignore the data that showed significant risk and consequences for users and for our society. In addition to the human cost, the societal cost of drug use impacts every taxpayer. The issue of legalizing pot was *not* merely a question of personal freedom.

When I was in Congress, I never voted to legalize recreational marijuana, but I had been in favor of medical marijuana, with proper guidance from doctors to individual patients. But a huge problem with legalizing this drug is that potency is not regulated, nor does it go through Food and Drug Administration review, so people do not really know the potency they're putting into their body. Genetic modification of the plants can also create extremely high THC count, which many proponents agree can be dangerous. Legalizing any drug could open up the state (which really means the taxpayers) to liability lawsuits.

Although I'm not a libertarian, I do believe adults should be free to make their own choices about life. But when those choices negatively impact others, that's where we need to draw the line. When it came to the issue of legalizing marijuana (which equates to promoting it), I actually practiced what all the COVID pundits preached: I trusted the science. And there was a lot of irrefutable science to trust, in addition to seeing how legalization impacted young people in other states.

ACT ONE: ON THE BALLOT

I was very clear that I'd personally vote against legalization of marijuana for recreational use. But hundreds of people who felt the same way inspired me to do more. I truly believed the constitutional amendment, if passed, would be harmful for *everyone* in our state on some level. Good leaders look forward, see possibilities and pitfalls, and tell people what they believe about the future.

The issue would probably be political baggage for me down the road—we were going against the tide on this issue. Ever since the Obama administration decided to ignore federal law and look the other way, more and more states were legalizing marijuana and creating a whole new industry.

Was normalizing marijuana inevitable? Was social decline inevitable? I didn't know, but I decided to see if I could help by doing some commercials, social media posts, and what seemed like dozens and dozens of meetings.

To complicate the matter, the ballot measures going before the voters included both recreational and medical use on the same ballot, and the bill's wording was quite confusing. In addition, the amendments added three new elements to our Constitution, which violated a constitutional provision the voters had passed just a few years before. (Only one element can be added at a time, according to our state Constitution.)

Both the medical and recreational marijuana amendments passed. The people voted for it.

ACT TWO: IN THE COURTS
We then faced the decision about whether to challenge the new *recreational* marijuana law on constitutional grounds, and did just that, which took over a year. On a 4-1 vote, the court agreed with our argument and threw out the new amendment—which had won the popular vote.

You can guess what unfolded politically. *Kristi Noem doesn't care about the will of the people.*

"She's a heartless dictator!" they shouted.

"The bill was unconstitutional," we replied. But you can guess which message received more traction. "I took an oath to uphold the Constitution. That's my job as governor." I then made it clear that if another bill was written constitutionally, and it passed, I would not stand in the way of it becoming law.

(By the way, we implemented a statewide medical cannabis program, which the voters had approved separately, in record time.)

ACT THREE: VOTE WITH YOUR HEART
After another year of wrangling, a new ballot measure (which seemed to be constitutional) was written and the statewide

vote was scheduled. Frankly, I was tired of all the legal wrangling and personal attacks. But despite that, I truly believed that promoting recreational drug use was wrong. Plain and simple. This fight wasn't personal, but I decided to make the factual case to the people based on science and let them decide.

Those promoting the bill spent a year and millions of dollars in advertising to win the hearts and minds of the voters. All the usual arguments were rolled out. *Poof! Magical tax revenues will appear in a cloud of smoke, and this money would fund wonderful programs.* Yeah, great programs like increased drug addiction counseling and more mental health services— to keep up with the needs that legalization would drive.

In town hall meetings across the state, I reminded everyone that "In the campaign I was clear about not wanting to legalize recreational marijuana. My position hasn't changed. But if this bill is constitutional, and passes, I won't oppose it." I will make sure the law is followed and implement it.

And then I took the argument straight to the consciences of our citizens.

"Is there any parent who says, 'I really hope when my kids grow up they'll really like marijuana'? I've never once met anybody who got smarter or more motivated by smoking dope. Have you?"

That line was quoted in the paper probably dozens of times. And some on my staff would remind me that it wasn't necessarily the most brilliant phrase. "Why are you calling it *dope*?" they'd ask.

"Because it sticks with people and gets repeated by the media!" I didn't really care if the line made me look silly as long as the message connected with the heart. My policy positions are probably more conservative than the average citizen in my state, if there's even such a thing as an "average" citizen. But I believe that I've never lost an election because people appreciate how I talk with them—even if we might disagree. Again, it's part of my commitment to talking moderately so we can govern conservatively.

As one of my staff recently pointed out in a meeting, whatever the elephant in the room is, I'm probably going to be the first one to talk about it. And while we're at it, I seem to have the keen ability to gravitate toward awkward conversations. At a recent event I grabbed one of many open seats among many tables. I didn't know anyone at the table, but I saw it as an opportunity to get to know a few new folks. I sat down, introduced myself, and asked them all their names. As they answered and we all shook hands, I started to ask where they lived and what they did for a living. I quickly learned that all the people sitting at this particular table ran marijuana growing facilities and distribution centers. Not exactly my biggest fans. But we had a great conversation and left that evening as new friends.

Just a few months ago, I went to a funeral in a nearby state and after attended a big lunch reception, full of friends and family. I decided to sit at a table full of strangers because I thought it might be nice to meet some new people. I just happened to choose a table with three educators, who, I could tell (because of my *amazing* powers of perception), were not big fans of me.

I could almost hear them groan when I asked, "Can I sit by you?" In some ways, it was probably the worst table I could have picked. But by the time we left, I think we were on our way to understanding each other more, and I was truly impressed with these amazing people who spend their lives investing in our youth. I hope they liked me a little better after our interaction as well.

I'm not sure if it's a gift or God having a wise sense of humor with me, but sometimes sitting down to visit with people who seem like political "enemies" and talking openly about issues brings surprising progress for everyone. At least that's my experience.

I guess I'm that way for a lot of reasons, but mainly because I have faith in people. I believe that when we pause and search our heart about a decision, we'll almost always go in a positive direction. And I happen to really like and respect the people I serve. They give me hope every day.

Back to the story.

As the debate wafted through our communities, we started to notice people wearing buttons with a photo of me and the words "In your heart, you know she's right." To this day I have no idea who made them, but they were everywhere. Evidently, my corny line about smoking dope made people stop and consider the issue in a fresh way.

The buttons are the perfect example of what can happen when elected leaders communicate clearly *and* when citizens get personally involved. Our team didn't brainstorm the idea, nor did a consultant at an ad agency create it; some concerned South Dakotans invested their own creativity, time, and money to change hearts and minds. (By the way, this isn't an isolated example. During campaigns I saw hundreds of homemade yard signs and even billboards supporting me.)

As the marijuana vote was tallied, the people of the state voted the recreational pot legalization measure down. Yes, our voters went from yes to no. And the difference was clear communication. I can have mud thrown at me by the press and the legislature every day, but for some reason, it doesn't seem to stick in the minds of our voters. Probably because they know me. I think they know my heart. I talk honestly with them. I listen with a desire to learn. And they appreciate it.

A few weeks ago, I texted Bryon and told him I was going to stop by the grocery store on the way home. He was at the gym, and an hour later when he finally looked at his phone, he told his friends, "Oh my gosh, I have to go. Kristi's at the grocery store!" When they asked why being at the store was such an emergency he answered, "Because I know she's swarmed and she'll never get out of there."

Sure enough, when he arrived I was chatting with about ten people around me, and I had just two items in my cart. Yeah, I'm the dummy who still thinks I can throw a ball cap on and have a quick stop for groceries. But this is my home state and hometown. This is one way I stay connected to the folks I serve. And I've learned to try not to be in a hurry. Folks appreciate a good visit at the grocery store.

CULTURE WAR?

As Joseph Heller wrote in *Catch-22*, "Just because you're paranoid doesn't mean they aren't after you."[3] The fact is, there really are forces working to tear down what we hold dear and move our country in a direction that is harmful.

This story about drugs can be applied to other moral, cultural, and constitutional issues of our time: abortion, energy, homelessness, immigration, education, law enforcement, religious expression, what books are in our libraries, and even foreign wars.

As we work together to address these issues, we must use wisdom and love. Yes, love.

Conservatives are often harsh and judgmental, but we were created to love each other. We must treat other people the way we hope to be treated. Yes, God created us to love each other and bring unity—not drive people away by condemning and arguing. We can put forth an argument for what we believe in, but people will be open to our views only if we draw them to us, if they like us, and if we give them hope. We should be happy—happy warriors for conservative values. That's how we stop the backward slide and move forward. I don't always do well remembering this in my communication—nobody does—but it's always my goal.

There she goes again, breaking the law of separation of church and state, and imposing her morals on others!

Despite what many misinformed people say about the Establishment Clause, the phrase "separation of church and state" does not appear in the First Amendment of the Constitution.

The actual text reads, "Congress shall make no law respecting an establishment of religion." And our founding documents were based on concepts of moral law, including those found in the Bible.

The United States government must not throw its weight and power behind a certain religion or sect, but that certainly doesn't mean the convictions you and I hold should be put on a shelf when it comes to stepping into the arena.

You're probably well aware that folks on the left do not hesitate for one second to impose their agenda on us. That's why we must *lead* the conversation, in order to lead our nation forward. A leader can't lead until they know exactly where they're going and are determined to stay the course.

When I was in Congress, after a vote one day I walked to the elevator, and in walked Democrat representative Charlie Rangel. (For younger readers who might not know the name, he represented districts in New York City from 1971 to 2017 and had a larger-than-life personality and natural charm.) "How's your day going today, Charlie?" I asked.

"I just met with Speaker Pelosi," he replied with a grin, in his trademark raspy voice. "I had to tell her, 'I was with you from the *beginning*. I'm with you *now*, and I will stay with you . . . *as long as I can be.*'"

I burst out laughing, because that's a perfect summation of commitment in DC—*I'll stay with you . . . as long as I can . . . until I can't be.*

I had to ask. "What'd she say to *that*?"

"Oh, she took *great* reassurance from it."

Perfect, right? With friends like that, who needs enemies. So as we look around at the forces conspiring against the values we hold dear, and look forward to our vision for America, let's remember how dysfunctional our political system is. The bad news is that we've been losing the culture war—losing to a mob with no real vision, questionable loyalties, and coercive "persuasion" tools.

The good news is that we can do better. We can overcome evil with good. (And yeah, that's in the Bible, in Romans 12:21.)

HAPPY WARRIORS

I love the wisdom of Arthur Brooks, and I've adapted one of his sayings into my own creed: great leaders never get angry on behalf of themselves; they get mad on behalf of others.

Whenever we speak up, we must stay focused on the issue at hand and the people it affects but never worry about what others say about us, personally. This helped me so much in the marijuana debate, and it helps me today.

For example, when I saw how many children in our state needed foster parents, I was astounded, sad, and angry. People didn't know we had a foster care recruiting shortage until we started educating the public. Kids were actually living and sleeping in state offices with our caseworkers, while they awaited a loving home to take them in when their family hit a crisis. In just one year, we recruited three hundred new families, which is a significant number for us. That made me happy—and a lot of other people got happy, too!

Let's get over ourselves, our offenses, and whatever other excuses are holding us back. Let's start talking with people about things that matter to our communities. We can disagree without being jerks. We can speak the truth in love (yep, another Bible idea) and see hearts and minds changed.

The same applies to social media. I admit, my social media posts are kind of fun and crazy, but sometimes . . . boring. But that's intentional. (I hope you'll follow me, though.) Compared to all the bomb throwing and clickbait in that world, my team and I *try* to stay focused on South Dakota and on national issues that affect us. Again, that's the winning strategy of continual education and communication.

CHURCH AND STATE

Can I share one more thing I'm angry about? I'm tired of listening to many Christians tell me it's the government's job to take care of people. It's actually our job as the church, and there are many ways we can do it. Yes, the government has a role in some important ways, but Christians aren't called to delegate the cross; we're called to carry it. How do we change this? Pastors must also communicate and educate.

I've spent countless hours *after* church services talking to people who have needs. Sometimes it feels like I should bring a staffer with us to handle all the casework that's brought to me. "Governor, can you help me get my unemployment check? Governor, can you help me get food stamps?" I want to help people. I do. And I always do what I can to assist. But in most situations, what people need, they could handle themselves or in partnership with church staff and local leaders. That's how life is supposed to work, in my view. Pastors must preach that provision comes from God and not government.

We're designed to work faithfully so we have the means to help others who genuinely need it.

I'm glad there are people praying for me and other leaders. Wow, I sure need it! But this world also needs people who step into the mess and become part of the solution. I enjoy yelling at my TV as much as anyone, but in reality it accomplishes zero. We can't delegate our God-given responsibility to bureaucrats. Clearly, it's a disaster when we try. Here's how Margaret Thatcher saw it.

"I think we have gone through a period when too many children and people have been given to understand 'I have a problem, it is the Government's job to cope with it!' or 'I have a problem, I will go and get a grant to cope with it!' 'I am homeless, the Government must house me!' and so they are casting their problems on society and who is society? There is no such thing! There are individual men and women and there are families, and no government can do anything except through people and people look to themselves first."[4]

Whether it's drugs or abortion or schools, forward progress doesn't just happen. It's really hard work. Maybe the hardest part is reaching out to people you don't normally hang out with and building a respectful relationship with them. One of the best things conservatives can do is volunteer in a community with very different views and let our actions speak.

There are many sincere Christians who are registered Democrats. The ones I know have a belief that their party is more compassionate, caring, and concerned about the poor and middle class. That might have been true a few decades ago, but not today. The challenge for you and me is to change their minds by our actions. Then more people will listen to our vision for the future.

STEP FORWARD

It's not the government's job to tell people what they can or can't do—unless someone's choices and consequences of those choices impact others in measurable ways. Then it's up to leaders to make their case with the people they serve—not simply issue executive orders and policy changes behind closed doors.

Electing good people is important, but we can't rely on elected officials to change the culture of our local community. People are culture, and people change culture, for better or worse.

The world is run by people—people who show up and don't give up. And believe me, when people speak up and show up, politicians take notice.

NINE

DONKEYS, RINOS, AND BISON

> There's a lot that I think Democrats are proud of that
> Joe Biden has been able to do. If Joe Biden were to
> quit right now, he'd be on Mount Rushmore.
> —Van Jones on CNN, December 2023[1]

> *I can't imagine endorsing anybody, and my
> endorsement would be the kiss of death.*
> —Mitt Romney, December 2023[2]

My mom's family had a lot of Democrats. Dad's family was mostly Republicans. Same situation when I married into the Noem family; quite a few of Bryon's relatives were Democrats, including his mom! Many people think South Dakota is very conservative, but in truth, we are much more populist. And, for the most part, we make it work.

When I was growing up, and even today, holiday gatherings were a time to focus on what we had in common and love each other, despite the fact that we knew there were many opposing political views around the table. Navigating these realities has made me a better person and a better leader. I have tried to find common ground around the table, and while our family has had a lot of tough discussions, we have mostly left the table respecting each other.

It seemed to me that traditionally, in the 1950s and a few decades thereafter, Democrats were often described as "caring" about farmers and blue-collar folks. Those allegiances are in the blood of many Americans. Ronald Reagan even began his political career as a Democrat. When he switched parties, he explained it like this: "I didn't leave the Democratic Party; the party left me."[3] (Just wait until you read what Democrats used to believe about education, in the next chapter.)

The challenge and great opportunity for Republicans today is that many longtime Democrats don't fully realize how much their party has changed. And unless we do a better job of communicating with them, they won't learn what we truly stand for as conservatives. As an elected official, it was never a problem working with Democrats. I grew up around them. They were my aunts, uncles, cousins, neighbors, and friends.

That said, I did learn a lot about getting along with people from my sister. She's the peacemaker in the family. I'm the arguer, but you already knew that. Our family has always worked together in our family business, and as in any business, changes, conflicts, and differences arise. When that happens, we have a choice to make. We all decided long ago that we value our relationships above all else. Yes, we are free to express our views. But family gatherings are family gatherings, not business meetings or debates.

Okay, that's enough about getting along with each other. :-)

Let's talk honestly about some of the characters we meet along the way.

DONKEYS

When Bryon and I were married, we moved to the ranch where we live now. I was twenty years old and still in college. That's when Dad decided to move the entire cattle herd to our ranch. Subtle message: he was done calving out cows. That meant that during calving season, Bryon and I would be checking on cows and their babies 24/7. I'd run the herd before, but this was different. Now, I had the full responsibility.

Our ranch is in what you might call "rougher" country, where coyotes are prolific. We were losing lots of calves to them, which was devastating to our livelihood. I told Dad I wanted to go out to Custer State Park and buy one of those burros or donkeys I'd heard about. Years earlier I read an article about how a donkey would protect a herd from coyotes. Dad said it was a silly idea—but the funny thing was, he offered to go along with me.

So we drove across the state to the buffalo auction, where they were also selling some donkeys. When it came time to bid, suddenly Dad became quite the expert. "No, you don't want that one. You want *that* one." We won the bidding on his choice animal and proceeded to load it into the trailer. This donkey wasn't trained but was characteristically stubborn. We had to lift each hoof up into the trailer, which was like hoisting tree stumps.

"This thing is not worth two bits," Dad said, which was the closest thing to swearing for him.

"Why did you pick that one?" I asked, as we drove home.

"Because I think she's pregnant. And you'll end up with two."

And I thought, *Here's the guy who couldn't believe I wanted one donkey, and now he made sure we would have two!*

Several months later, Two Bit (yeah, that's what I named her) had a foal, and over the years she had several more for us, including one we named Chachi. We put each into its own pasture, and they protected our herd for decades. Chachi is still with us and has quite the collection of selfies. Every Republican who visits the ranch gets their photo taken with him, as proof that they can get along with a "big D" donkey.

Here's something else we learned working with those animals. If you have just one donkey in a field, they'll protect your cows and chase off predators. But if you have two or more together, they stop caring about the herd they're supposed to protect. Instead, they just hang around each other and are pretty much worthless.

It wouldn't be a huge stretch to draw a parallel between this story and some of my experiences working with Democrats. I've had countless one-on-one conversations with members of the Democratic Party, and we usually agree on important matters for our constituents and get stuff done.

But sometimes it seems like when donkeys group together they stop caring about our little ones. Sadly, that's happened way too often in recent years when it comes to abortion, educational standards, safe communities, border security, and protecting kids from harmful sexual ideology. When the donkeys only care about each other, children suffer.

ASS BACKWARD

It seems most Democrats keep walking backward, despite the term "progressive."

Is it *progress* to exclude someone from adopting children because they believe boys and girls are different? That's what was alleged in Oregon last year, in this statement from the attorneys handling the case: "The Oregon Department of Human Services [. . .] denied her application because Bates would not agree to say and do things that conflict with her faith, like facilitating a child's access to dangerous drug interventions that block their natural, biological development, taking children to Pride parades, or using pronouns inconsistent with a child's sex."[4] Why do so many Democrats seem obsessed with the sexuality of children?[5]

Does it sound like progress to have the federal government actively work to undermine the efforts of southern states that are trying to secure their border? Maybe you saw the recent images of the US Border Patrol—under orders from the Biden administration—cutting away razor wire that Texas had placed in their efforts to deter illegal immigration.

Last year, it came to our attention that a female member of the South Dakota National Guard was forced to bunk and shower with a man who identified as a woman, during basic training with the US Army.[6] We did all we could to intervene but, in the end, federal rules and woke bureaucracy made it clear that her only options were to accept the sad new realities of our military or resign.

When you think about progressives, maybe you'll agree that their policies make life less free and more expensive. In fact, a 2023 study by the Competitive Enterprise Institute found that US households pay almost $15,000 per year in hidden regulatory costs.[7] Couple that with Biden-flation, and you could claim that Democrat policies are actually *regressive.*

I wonder how many Democrats realize that their party actually prohibited other Democrats from competing with

President Biden in the 2024 election primary?[8] Yes, that's democracy now, in their world. But it sounds more like Russia and China.

Did you know that in 2021 the Democrat-leaning National School Boards Association worked with the White House to have the FBI investigate parents—who they outrageously compared to "domestic terrorists"—for opposing critical race theory in their kids' schools?[9] After a huge outcry, the association apologized for the language in the letter. But the Department of Justice still deployed resources.

I could write an entire book full of this nonsense. Does anyone know what "progressive" means anymore? (Teddy Roosevelt was a progressive!) The word means something different to everyone, and maybe that's why the left clings to that deceptive label. But I see more and more Democrats waking up to the fact that today's Democratic Party is unrecognizable compared to thirty years ago.

WORKING WITH DONKEYS

As a state representative, I worked closely with a wonderful colleague, Democrat state senator Jim Peterson, to help rewrite the property tax code in South Dakota. I don't know why he was a Democrat; maybe because his parents and grandparents were. But we never talked about party politics. We simply agreed that the current taxation scheme was outdated and unfair to many citizens. Jim had put forth similar legislation previously, but I decided to cosponsor the bill with him one year, and you could hear people's heads exploding all over the state.

What the hell is that upstart Republican doing, sponsoring a bill with a longtime Democrat?

Several Democrats and Republicans were outraged—not because of the merits of the proposal, but because someone from the "other party" was working on it. Instead of just dismissing the bill for petty partisan reasons, legislators had to actually read the bill and debate it.

The legislation eventually passed in a version very similar to the original proposal that Jim and I worked on. Citizens benefitted. What a concept!

But I have a few stories that turned out differently. Democrat Tim Walz was a member of Congress from Minnesota, and we worked closely on conservation bills, like on the Conservation Reserve Program and the farm bill. We shared many of the same values and policy concerns. Years later, we both ran for governor of our respective states and both won. During COVID, let's just say we had different views.[10] He was pretty vocal in his criticism of me. It seemed that he did a complete 180 in terms of fighting for the people he represented.

In a *totally* unrelated decision, I decided to direct significant portions of our business recruitment ad budget to billboards in Minnesota, with this invitation: "Move to South Dakota for freedom." One of the billboards we chose was very close to the governor's mansion—not coincidentally, of course. We knew he'd have to drive by them and see them every day. Just the thought of it still makes me chuckle.

But it was no accident that many families moved from his state to ours.

RINOS MOONWALKING

You probably know what a RINO is—someone who's a Republican In Name Only. In other words, they wear the GOP label but don't act like an elephant at all.

As governor, I delivered the largest tax cut in South Dakota history. A previous governor passed the largest tax increase in South Dakota history. And we're both Republicans.

RINOs (and rhinos) don't have very good vision, are quite irritable, and will charge when they feel threatened. But they're quite talented, too—RINOs can *moonwalk*, appearing to go forward while actually drifting backward to the 1990s and 2000s.

How do you spot one? Just watch how they vote, whom they endorse, and whom they attack.

But don't be fooled. RINOs are much more dangerous than most people think. In many ways, these political creatures are worse than some donkeys. RINOs are complicit in the decline of our country and standing in the way of positive change. They seem nostalgic about the corruption and insider policies of decades past. People like Mitt Romney and Liz Cheney bring division and damage what we want the Republican brand to stand for. Instead of working together to identify problems that are destroying our nation, RINOs bicker.

The Republican Party is the answer to the challenges of today, but only if we remain true to our principles and follow through on our promises to the people. And we must convey our message in a way that brings hope. Our world is desperate for optimism and solutions that work.

LOBBYISTS IN THE CAPITOL LOBBY
Most Americans know the term "lobbyist," but few know what it means. So, let's fix that with a basic overview.

Ninety percent of lobbyists are not brilliant people—in my experience, anyway. But wow, do they influence what happens and doesn't happen in government. And the 10 percent that are smart? Watch out for them.

Who are these people? They're former elected officials or their staffers. A "successful" lobbyist is paid a lot of money because of their network of relationships and their ability to set up meetings. And sometimes the most successful lobbyists are those who just show up and tell their story.

The most effective lobbying I ever saw while in Congress was in the morning of a day when my colleagues and I were going to vote on a government funding bill. The bill was basically done and sure to pass, but several amendments were set to be voted on.

One was funding for juvenile diabetes research. My standard answer, as a good Republican, was to be skeptical about any last-minute provisions. After all, I was there to help *curb* spending, and I knew we were already funding billions in all kinds of important medical research.

Cue the Juvenile Diabetes Research Foundation lobby and the hundreds of precious kids they brought along to meet us. A few of those little kiddos sat down with me, opened up their scrapbooks, and started showing me what their life was like in pictures. "Here's how many times a day I get a shot." "This is my mom, and she must go to school with me because we don't have a school nurse. She sits with me all day long to check my blood, because we can't afford to get a pump."

I also have some family members with type 1 diabetes, so I knew something about the hardships these families endured. As I walked to the House to vote that afternoon, every member of Congress had one subject on their mind. "Did those juvenile diabetes kids come see you today?" "Oh my gosh, I am *so* voting for that amendment." It passed overwhelmingly, with no pushback. And I'm glad.

Here's a tip for lobbyists: facts are important, but stories are crucial. (That's also a free tip for elected leaders and their communications teams.)

The point isn't that lobbying is bad; it's that lobbying works. But people need to lobby for themselves once in a while! I tell my legislature that all the time: "This place is filled with lobbyists. They get paid to be here. Who lobbies for the taxpayer? *Our* job is to lobby for the people who aren't here, because they're working hard and raising families, and trying to stay ahead of the bureaucracy."

BACK TO THE NINETIES?

Donald Trump definitely disrupted the donkeys and RINOs. And he still is a burr under their saddles. In December 2023, Paul Ryan, the former House speaker, said, "And so I think Adam [Kinzinger] and Liz [Cheney] stepped out of the flow and called it out and, you know, paid for it. Paid for it with their careers."[11]

I understand that Paul Ryan and President Trump have different approaches and perspectives, but I can't help but notice Ryan's concern for the "careers" of politicians—like somehow elected officials have some sort of tenure, or right to stay in power. I wonder if President George Washington ever envisioned the idea of career politicians. His remarks in his farewell address seem to say so.

In his farewell address of 1796, Washington warned us, "However [political parties] may now and then answer popular ends, they are likely, in the course of time and things, to become potent engines by which cunning, ambitious, and unprincipled men will be enabled to subvert the power of the people and to usurp for themselves the reins of government, destroying afterwards the very engines which have lifted them to unjust dominion."[12]

Here's my paraphrase to twenty-first-century language, if I may: "Politicians may occasionally do some good, but in the process, they'll amass connections and power. The temptation is always there to forget about the people they serve and use that power for their own selfish ambitions. The result will be the destruction of our republic."

It's time for elected leaders of both parties to focus on the people they serve, wake up to our nation's decline, and do something to turn it around. Donald Trump entered the arena and asked questions Republicans weren't even thinking about.

"Why do we have to close our steel factories?"

"Why wouldn't we secure our border?"

"Why not put America first?"

The Republican Party must be the party of freedom. Republicans must roll back Joe Biden's assault on the Bill of Rights, freedom of speech, freedom of assembly, freedom of religion, the right to bear arms, and the ability of the states to decide on their own issues.

As then Supreme Court justice Louis Brandeis famously said in the early 1900s, "The states are the laboratories of democracy."[13] Our states should be examples for the nation, enacting conservative reforms and proving our policies create more success and opportunity for our people.

It matters who's in charge. And as a party, we as Republicans will have failed if we do not make our case about the consequences of having Democrats and RINOs in charge.

BE THE BISON

In 2013, winter storm Atlas raged across South Dakota and neighboring states and left thousands and thousands of cattle dead. It was a tragedy on many levels. But interestingly, stories emerged about how many bison survived the horrendous rain, snow, and wind.

Unlike the cattle, who often followed each other, pushed by the winds into deathtraps of snow-drifted fencing and bluffs, the bison stood and faced the blizzard. Many ranchers reported that the bison walked *into* the storm. I've seen this at our ranch, while cattle move away, or face away, from bad weather and wind, bison stand firm. Their natural instinct is to face adversity. They know that if they face the storm and keep moving forward, they will move through the crisis sooner.

America needs fewer RINOs, and I hope the Democratic Party continues to shrink, as it has in many states.[14] But what we really need are more *bison*—citizens who can face adversity, walk into the storm, and stand strong.

By the way, we have over fifteen hundred wild bison here in South Dakota's Custer State Park. They're truly amazing creatures, and I hope you'll visit them.

MAKE VOTING TRUSTWORTHY AGAIN

"In the USA, you don't need government issued ID to vote and you can mail in your ballot. This is insane," Elon Musk posted on X in January 2024.[15]

I agree, Elon. But our election system—ballots and polling—in South Dakota has integrity. Citizens vote on or shortly before Election Day. Voter identification is required. And there are some limitations around switching parties, so people won't try to influence the outcome of a primary to get a certain candidate through who is beatable in a general election.

We have no ballot drop boxes or mail-in balloting. Absentee balloting is available for our military and for certain individuals.

Our state limits private dollars funding election operations. But in 2022 I proposed the "Zuck Bucks" bill to prevent private money from funding election operations, and it passed. I was proud to sign it into law here in our state.[16] The bill got its name from Mark Zuckerberg and his wife, who contributed $350 million to various election offices across the nation in 2020 alone. "Elections should be funded by the government, and we will not risk creating avenues for big-tech billionaires to unfairly influence our free and open elections," I said at the time.

We vote on paper ballots, and they're all counted. We have tabulating machines, but they are not connected to the internet. Both Democrats and Republicans have conducted nefarious activities to manipulate election results across the nation. That's why I believe we need a paper trail to guarantee accurate counts and recounts.

If voting doesn't look like this where you live, talk to your governor. And there's someone else you should get to know: your secretary of state. In most states, this elected office is responsible for the processes, integrity, and transparency of the election system. Yet most people simply don't know who their secretary of state is.

Here's something concrete you can do in your state. Ask your secretary of state what they're doing to make sure the voter rolls are cleaned up for accuracy. Trust me, dead people "vote"—and they especially like mail-in ballots. Another big issue is duplicate ballots, created for the same person, because of name changes over the years. It happened in several states in 2020, where someone received multiple ballots. They may have received one under their maiden name, then another with their married name or after a divorce. Differences occur, and multiple ballots are generated depending on when and how the full name is recorded, changed, or even spelled—but never deleted in the system. Mary Smith got a ballot, Mary Anne Smith got one, and so did Mary Smith Jones, and they're all the same person.

While you're checking with your new BFF (the secretary of state) about the voter rolls, ask them about how they verify identification for a person to vote. It's just stupid if they tell you they can't figure out a way to make our elections secure and accurate. It's not complicated or difficult.

WINNING IS BETTER

Losing sucks. But Republicans happen to be great at it, often when it seems to matter most. And I believe the main reason is our party's lack of a communication strategy that's clear and relatable. Again, the Democrats usually do a better job of talking with people. A pretty famous television celebrity and producer recently said to me in a casual conversation, "Republicans never miss an opportunity to miss an opportunity."

Since I became governor in 2018, no Republican leader asked me to come to a district to help a representative get elected. But I've probably helped fifty across the country because they personally asked me. Where is our Republican leadership when it comes to leveraging other members of our party to help win, and keep, majorities in the House and Senate?

For several years, including in early 2023, I asked then House Speaker Kevin McCarthy to consider creating a communication "SWAT team" and have them travel to states and districts that needed a boost. The team would be made up of four or five people who were excellent communicators (governors, cabinet members, and members of Congress, for example) and would make the case for the party, legislative issues, and particular candidates.

Not only would the team's individual voices make a difference, but the impact of a coalition—different people from different bodies and levels of elected office with a united message—would be a game changer. When's the last time you saw a governor and a senator and a congressperson doing events and press conferences together—or doing anything together? And the team could also "cover" for local candidates, saying what needed to be said. He didn't seem interested and after multiple conversations, I quit asking. Senators weren't interested. The party wasn't interested. But I think it was an opportunity missed.

I'll keep doing what I can on an individual basis, but imagine what a unified team of voices could do to change the game in every state!

STEP FORWARD

We are a family—this weird, amazing family called America.

Let's decide to love each other, talk with each other, and be honest. Both parties have changed over the years. But what you and I do and say will frame what the Republican Party stands for going forward.

Talk to some old donkeys and RINOs about the way forward. Have a conversation with those "unde-cided" and independent voters. Yes, there are many areas in which we disagree, but with most people there's a lot more that we agree on.

———o———————————o———

FREEDOM OF SPEECH AND EDUCATION

They have not one thing that they offer as a solution
other than privatizing or voucher-izing schools which
is about undermining democracy and undermining
civil discourse and undermining pluralism because
90 percent of our kids go to public schools still [. . .]
They just divide. Divide. Divide. Divide.

—RANDI WEINGARTEN, PRESIDENT OF THE AMERICAN
FEDERATION OF TEACHERS[1]

*The philosophy of the school room in one generation
will be the philosophy of government in the next.*

—QUOTE ATTRIBUTED TO ABRAHAM LINCOLN

S eems to me, more scrutiny is given to the food served in
school cafeterias than the books provided to kids in
our school libraries.

My first two years of college, I was studying to become an
elementary schoolteacher. Our kids went to public school,

and many people in my extended family are teachers. I love kids and respect good teachers.

When we consider the future of our nation, education must be a cornerstone. As Abraham Lincoln reportedly noted, we can tell what our government will be like by looking at our classrooms today. Honestly, I see a lot of good and bad—encouraging and frightening.

So, how did we get here? And, most importantly, what can we do to improve education for our kids?

GREAT EXPECTATIONS

Read these words from an American president's state of the union address, only a few years ago: "I challenge every state to give all parents the right to choose which public school their children will attend, and to let teachers form new schools with a charter they can keep only if they do a good job.

"I challenge all our schools to teach *character* education, to teach good values and good citizenship.

"And if it means that teenagers will stop killing each other over designer jackets, then our public schools should be able to require their students to wear school uniforms.

"I challenge our *parents* to become their children's first teachers. Turn off the TV. See that the homework is done. And visit your children's classroom. No program, no teacher, no one else can do that for you."

Wow. School choice. Morality and citizenship. Uniforms. And an emphasis on the most important people in a child's life—parents. Sounds like a wonderful, workable vision to turn education around, and seems like a MAGA platform. But those words were actually delivered by President Bill Clinton, in his 1996 State of the Union address.[2] *Yes really.*

Back then there were a few donkeys advocating for the best possible educational opportunities. What the heck happened? There are many reasons for this decline in expectations, but here's a story that's quite telling.

NO CHILD LEFT BEHIND?

When I ran for the state legislature, I campaigned as a mom and businessperson. After I won the election, I introduced a bill to increase minimum teacher salaries. At the time, this was quite controversial, but South Dakota was at the bottom of the country in terms of what teachers earned. There was a shortage of teachers but, interestingly, not a shortage of cash.

Before the legislative session, every education lobbyist organization was on board, as you might imagine. "Of course, we will testify and help this bill become law!" Seemed like smooth sailing ahead. But the night before the bill went to committee, they all backed out. Why? Because I had insisted that we weren't going to tie teacher salary increases to more money for schools. Even though our school districts enjoyed historic budget reserves, they refused to support the raises because the bureaucracy wouldn't also get a "raise."

I remember going to the committee that morning where I'd been expecting the fifteen people who had committed to testify to do so—and realizing I would have to go it alone. And not only that, but my previous teammates in this mission now all testified against the bill! It was a close vote in committee, but the power of the "education" lobby had an impact, and my bill died by one vote.

At the end of the day, it was all about more money—not for the teachers, but for the overall budgets and layers of management. That was a real teaching moment for me as a new legislator. Who really cares about teachers? It's not the lobby-ists or the unions. Few truly lobby for the most important people in the education process: the teacher, the student, and, of course, the parent.

The bill finally passed, with help from the Blue-Ribbon Task Force that was tied to the largest tax increase in the states' history, but the minimum teacher salary had no real teeth to it. Several school districts today still are not meeting the "goals" of the policy. In fact, we're still working to imple-ment new laws that will help our schools hire and retain the best teachers.

When I got to Congress, I served on the Education and Workforce Committee, and worked on federal education pol-icy including amendments to No Child Left Behind, which was a 2001 Republican initiative to address failing schools. I'm sure the original measure was well intentioned, but there were massive failures.

The consequences of this federal mandate were a mixed bag, in my view. A lot of what was in this legislation did more to hurt the students than to help them. Teachers and adminis-trators focused on "teaching for the test" because they were incentivized in ways that didn't necessarily create better learning for individual children in the classrooms. No Child Left Behind created a generation of test takers, while problem solving and critical thinking were "left behind."

It just goes to remind everyone the federal government is very rarely the answer to fixing our problems, let alone our problems in the classrooms.

In December 2023, two Republicans in Congress intro-duced the ACE Act, which would double the tax savings to parents who want options for their children's education. The bill would also incentivize states that remove barriers to school choice. That sort of federal legislation could help. Here are some details, with apologies for some wonky language.

The proposal doubles 529 tax-exempt account distributions from $10,000 per taxable year to $20,000 per year, provides gift tax exclusions of up to $20,000 per taxable year for placement in 529 accounts, and varies federal tax exemption amounts to incentivize states with school choice laws.[3] Of course, this bill, and others like it, will not see the light of day unless the 2024 election goes in favor of freedom.

EDUCATION IS LOCAL

Most school administrators and unions will not move education forward. A significant number of school boards are also part of the problem, in some cases trying to silence parents and limit access to information, although there are encouraging signs that this is changing. And it all points to the true solution to improve our public schools: the fact that parents are the real experts.

Over the past decades, the more power and control we gave to government education, the less our kids benefitted. The "experts" believed that parents couldn't be trusted to decide what the curriculum looks like because "they're not educated enough." And in many cases, school boards and administrators actively withhold information from parents.[4]

The only way to stop the decline and improve our schools is to get involved. But coincidentally, the establishment has made getting involved difficult and confusing. Parents and grandparents who show up at meetings are often greeted with procedural double-talk and passive-aggressive attitudes. After all, the boards and administrators "know best."

When a parent is newly elected to a school board, they enter a world of endless meetings and documents to research. Administrators present towering stacks of budget documents, along with assurances that their recommendations are solid. "Okay *(thud)*, this was our budget last year, which was approved. Based on that, here's this year's proposed budget— along with salary negotiations. Oh, and the principal already approved the curriculum."

If you've never served on a board or been part of a bureaucratic machine, the experience can be daunting or downright intimidating. And the rules are sometimes created to stifle questions. And astoundingly, some school boards have limited the frequency and allotted times for public comment at meetings. That's why, since I've been governor, I've been working to create a training program for all school board members. I know, continuing education for those who make crucial choices in our schools is a radical concept. Guess who opposes this concept? Yes, the establishment.

Every school board member, and especially new ones, should be empowered to know their legal authority, the personal liability they expose themselves to when taking the job, and what other stakeholders are required to bring to the table. The more information a school board member has, the better questions they'll be able to ask. Parents and grandparents are busy, and the system is rigged in favor of those with insider knowledge. And be aware that some resources, like the parent-teacher association, can serve as nothing more than extensions of the unions and administrators.

If there's one practical step I'd recommend to you and your friends, it would be to simply attend a school board meeting. Just listen, take notes, and familiarize yourself with the system. Then you'll be able to talk with family and friends about important issues and be more prepared to speak up and ask questions at future meetings. And by the way, your school board should not be meeting in an "executive session" unless they're discussing contractual and HR issues.

Ask questions and demand transparency, especially on where they are spending money. Parents need to hold school boards accountable that they are directing money where it impacts learning the greatest: in the classroom. And it's your money they're spending!

Trust me, just showing your face in that room will make a big impression.

In at least two instances in 2023, leftist school board members chose to be sworn in on a stack of sexually explicit books.[5] If these people are so bold about their agenda, shouldn't we be twice as bold when we stand up for what's right for our kids?

WHO ALLOWS THESE BOOKS?

As you've probably noticed, a lot of very questionable books end up in school libraries. Some are pure evil. I asked our Secretary of Education how that happens, and he informed me that certain "book clubs" and authors sometimes send boxes of free books. In other instances, these books are part of a curriculum subscription that the school has chosen, which also gives the impression to librarians and other administrators that the books are approved by their district.

The standard operating procedure at some schools is to simply make it available to kids—and of course "busyness" plays a role. The governor's office has limited power in many areas of education, but school boards have all the power they need—if we have the right people.

IT'S THE HISTORY, STUPID!

My kids were in high school when I was in Congress serving on the Education and Workforce Committee. We'd talk about what they discussed in their government and history classes.

"Do you guys ever talk about American history?" I asked one day.

They told me there were a few weeks on the subject, but it wasn't a major topic. At the time, the kids informed me that the major topic discussed was what everyone did last weekend and how the school's sports teams had performed. That really bothered me. (And I know, I was just preaching about attending school board meetings, and I wasn't going to the ones in my district. Maybe you'll give me a pass, since I was in DC a lot during those years.)

When I ran for governor in 2018, one of my pledges was to put more civics and history in our classroom. In my first State of the State speech, I told everyone that I'd be asking the legislature to pass a bill requiring every high school student to pass a citizenship test in order to graduate—basic information about America's history, our Constitution, and our republic. Even though the test is simple, takes about ten minutes, and is what legal immigrants are required to pass to become a citizen, you'd have thought I was calling for every kid—and their teacher—to climb Mount Everest in order to get a diploma.

Again, when commonsense proposals are put forth, it's very revealing who objects. In fact, it was Republicans—some of the RINO variety—who killed the bill. They said it wasn't necessary, and we shouldn't tell our schools what to teach or what curriculum to use. Opponents claimed it would be too much of a burden on the students and teachers. I was shocked. How could they not see what was happening in our schools and how little of our history our students were required to learn?

Two years later, after COVID had awakened parents to what was really happening—and not happening—in their schools, it was time for the education social studies standards to be renewed, which happens every seven years. That's when we removed the broken model and replaced it with the most conservative, history-based social studies standards in the country. We focused on a true, honest, and factual accounting of our nation's history. We discussed both our triumphs and our failures—and how we can learn from both. No agenda. Just the truth and the facts of the history of our state, our cultures, and our great nation.

Once again, it was parents and grandparents who made the difference in establishing these changes. They pushed back against the "experts" who were fighting to keep the status quo. These parents used common sense to demand better for their children. We received criticism from liberals and the media for not simply handing over the reform process to the education establishment.

We also started holding educational development conferences with our teachers and history teachers to take part in a tour of South Dakota to see many of the remarkable historic sites, like Wounded Knee and where Lewis and Clark crossed the Missouri River. These trips, and the fact that it's just teachers talking to teachers, have given them more opportunities to see these incredible sites themselves and helped them become more passionate about our history, which greatly impacts our kids.

If kids never get a true and honest concept of their history, our culture breaks down. When people don't have basic facts and understanding about the past, they'll fall for fake narratives and propaganda every time.

It's my dream that every child in this country hears some version of this truth on a regular basis: You woke up this morning in the United States of America. Simply because you're here, you are already more blessed than 99 percent of all the people in the world who have ever lived. Because you woke up here, in a country founded on life, liberty, and the pursuit of happiness, you have more opportunity than most people on the planet.

What a great way to start the day! And it's a reminder of the truth for every adult, as well. And while I'm dreaming, wouldn't it be amazing to hear this sentiment from more of our leaders?

HOMESCHOOL FREEDOM

In the early days of the COVID pandemic, many folks across the country started looking at moving to South Dakota, and they'd comment on my social media posts saying what they liked about our state. I also heard from folks who said things like "I'd love to move there, but . . ." There were two main "buts."

Number one was the weather (which is something we can never change, but it's really not as bad as some might imagine—and it's much better than North Dakota!). Number two was that they thought our homeschool laws were too strict, and I knew that we could do something about that.

In 2021, to improve support and opportunities for homeschool families, we empowered parental choice in education by bringing legislation to streamline homeschool requirements. Before that in 2019, I signed a bill making homeschool students eligible, on an equal basis, for the South Dakota Opportunity Scholarship. This scholarship provides up to $6,500 over four years to qualifying students who attend South Dakota colleges, tech schools, and universities.

It worked! Last summer I was walking our dog early in the morning when a van pulled over and stopped in front of me. A lady jumped out and came running down the street toward me. I didn't recognize her, but noticed the van was full of kids.

"Governor! Is that you? We just moved here, and I thought I recognized you. We're moving here because you support homeschoolers and for the policies you have here!" This family represented thousands of people who have moved here for freedom, support, and the ability to educate their children how they saw fit, free of woke ideology.

It's a recurring theme whenever you want to move an important issue forward: those opposing this freedom and common sense will fight you. But I'm grateful to the parents and elected leaders who made these improvements possible.

HISTORICAL PROGRESS IS POSSIBLE

My goal is to give each individual child in South Dakota the best possible education for their specific needs. This means ensuring our schools are relying on the input and guidance of *parents*—who know better than anyone else what's best for their kids. Here are a few accomplishments that our team, along with engaged parents, made possible so far.

We brought legislation to *ban* critical race theory and action civics in all South Dakota schools and universities.

When the legislature failed to pass the K–12 critical race theory ban, I issued an executive order instructing the Department of Education to review training, policies, and all materials that may promote divisive concepts. We *banned* the state Department of Education from receiving federal grants that require the teaching of critical race theory. I also directed the South Dakota Board of Regents, the governing body for the state's public universities, to do away with campus diversity offices.

We expanded school choice for parents by increasing the amount of money that went into our tax credit scholarship program, allowing more parents to send their children to the school of their choice, to do what's best for their child.

We revamped our social studies standards for K–12 to ensure that our students are taught our nation's history in a way that is fair, honest, true, and patriotic. My team worked with leading professionals to develop these criteria. The Heritage Foundation later described our social studies standards as perhaps the best in the country.

To promote scholarships and school choice, in 2022 I signed legislation expanding the Partners in Education Tax Credit Program, which funds in-state K–12 private school scholarships for low-income students from $2 million per year to $3.5 million per year.

In various roles serving the people in my state, my goal has been to make public education the best it can be and give parents opportunities to choose what they want for their kids. After all, parents know what's best for their child.

STEP FORWARD

When I was first elected to the state legislature years ago, I had a neighbor give some perspective that I've remembered to this day. He said, "Remember, Kristi, every day you're in legislative session, our way of life is in jeopardy." The message was clear. What we do matters. What we don't do matters.

I'm sorry to say that conservatives and independents have contributed to the decline in public education in two ways. We haven't shown up at meetings that matter. And when we have shown up, too often our voices are more angry than they are informed.

Believe me, I'm all for passionate debate and standing against the establishment. But the progress we've seen in our state has come from increased engagement and increased knowledge on the part of parents.

Attend some meetings and make the establishment a little nervous. Speak up with informed questions and opinions, and make them *a lot* nervous.

We can't delegate our future to "experts" or officials; we've seen what happens when we try. Yes, stepping into the fray is inconvenient and can feel awkward. But take courage from what Dana Perino's college speech coach said: "It's okay to have butterflies in your stomach, as long as you make them fly in formation."[6]

Children need *your* time, *your* questions, *your* voice. There's no substitute.

ELEVEN

THE MOST POWERFUL
PERSON IN GOVERNMENT

This is rural rage [. . .] and the regular guy in the
country goes, 'there they are snarling and making
fun of us again' and every time we make fun of
Trump, we're making fun of them . . . It's a weird
thing, but in a way it's like fighting terrorism.

—CHRIS MATTHEWS, DECEMBER 2023[1]

A government that cares about you tries to elevate
you. [. . .] Anyone who's trying to make you
dependent is trying to hurt you.

—TUCKER CARLSON[2]

S ome political leaders live in a *very different* world from
ordinary people. This is true from the school board to
city hall, to Congress, to the governor's residence.

Here's just one example: I got up this morning, answered
some important texts and emails from my team, and then hit
the gym with a group of friends and enjoyed conversation
about normal life stuff. After getting ready for the day, I had a

quick breakfast, eggs and bacon, and did a couple early interviews before heading out the door to the office.

At the office, I read my daily press briefing email, which recaps the good, bad, and ugly in the media, along with suggestions from my team on how we can put forth the facts or respond to certain stories if necessary. The next several hours zoomed by in meetings, and I also conducted calls with our team and others across the state about important decisions and initiatives. As usual, these issues required questions for our legal team, followed by updates on the status of who's suing our state today and all the battles we're fighting in court. I then went into scheduled meetings in the office or businesses to cap off the morning schedule.

While it is rare for me to escape for lunch, today was different. I went to a local favorite for takeout. There, I had the opportunity to talk with the cashier about the weather forecast and our South Dakota State Jackrabbits. As I looked around, I saw a lot of happy people going about their day, enjoying a thriving economy, 1.8 percent unemployment, and safe streets. *Weird, right?*

Didn't they know there was an epic battle raging on X about my latest interview on CBS? *How could these people even function?!*

Here's the reality: most of my days are spent in the reality of politics, which is very different from the reality of the rest of the world.

When I deliver speeches, I try to include stories I hear from the people I meet. I don't think people realize the impact they can make by showing up at a meeting, saying hello after a speech, and telling me how their everyday lives are impacted by what the government is and isn't doing. Countless positive initiatives have been sparked because of a simple comment from someone I met when I was out and about in our communities.

Recently, I had a free hour and went to get my nails done in Sioux Falls. I ended up having the best conversation and interaction with a young man. Apparently he's a hip hop artist and pro-marijuana, but we didn't even discuss pot; we just chatted, like normal people do. He asked if he could take a photo with me, and I was happy to.

A few hours later, Congressman Jason Smith, chairman of the House Ways and Means Committee from Missouri, texted me with an Instagram link to this artist's post, which included the caption "Babe said she made a mistake. Go listen to my new single, Roll it up!"

Maybe he was making fun of me, or maybe he also enjoyed the conversation. It didn't matter. I laughed, and his post made my day. Besides, I'm no dope, and of course the track was about making his own cigarettes . . .

Seriously, these are the moments I love about my job. That's what America is about. It's not about yelling and attacking each other on social media for the sake of clicks, likes, or views.

It constantly surprises me how much of my job is traditional "retail politics." In other words, most people believe that the government is layers and layers of bureaucracy that insulates you from the real world—and real people. That is the case, unless you intentionally take time to have conversations with people who don't live and breathe politics.

Because it's my nature to enjoy conversations with people after events, my staff has learned to schedule additional time for me after events to socialize. My message to other leaders is, don't be in such a hurry that you lose contact with reality. A three-minute conversation with someone could change your whole policy outlook in a much-needed way.

It's also one of the greatest aspects of being a governor. When someone tells me about a situation happening in the state, I can help get it resolved quickly. I have found out about more problems with state government from these quick conversations that I ever thought possible. My team loves it when I tell them about these interactions because they know we'll work to fix the issues—fast. That's what a good executive does: listens and then works to solve the problem.

ASK

In my early twenties, I simply started going to meetings to learn how agricultural policies were being made. I was a farmer and rancher, and ag policy had a direct impact on how we lived our lives. In those gatherings, something strange started to happen. People started asking, "Who is this young lady in these meetings with a lot of older farmers?" Before you knew it, I went from simply showing up, taking notes, and asking questions to being asked to serve on the South Dakota Soybean Association.

As you get more involved in your community, remember that attending a meeting doesn't necessarily mean you'll end up in a leadership position. Being the one who asks others to step up is equally important. I would have never run for office if people hadn't asked me to. Future leaders need support, and reluctant leaders need to be asked. When they ask you, say yes.

That's the way we move forward, with a friendly nod to history—a time when most people recognized that they needed to be part of the solution. Remember what John F. Kennedy famously said in his 1961 inaugural address:

> And so, my fellow Americans: ask not what your country can do for you—ask what you can do for your country.
>
> My fellow citizens of the world: ask not what America will do for you, but what together we can do for the freedom of man.
>
> Finally, whether you are citizens of America or citizens of the world, ask of us here the same high standards of strength and sacrifice which we ask of you. With a good conscience our only sure reward, with history the final judge of our deeds, let us go forth to lead the land we love, asking His blessing and His help, but knowing that here on earth God's work must truly be our own.[3]

In case you missed my point and President Kennedy's, the power to change our nation does not reside in Washington, DC, in your state capital, or at town hall. Please believe me, as someone who has had the honor of serving in various capacities: you hold the power. Your voice matters more than you realize. That's why the establishment is so bent on silencing you. And if you are silent, those around you are more likely to be silent. This applies to government meetings, dinner table conversations, and ball games.

Is DC corrupt and wasteful and dysfunctional because those leaders and influencers are corrupt? Maybe. Or maybe it's because people like us stopped speaking up.

Remember, they live in an alternate reality, and unless we give them a dose of our realities, they'll stay in la-la land.

KID STUFF

In my ideal world, every day would be "take your kids to work day"—and would also include grandkids! A woman can dream.

Yes, I believe children need some understanding of what adults do in the real world. (This need is painfully clear when you see viral videos of college graduates horrified at the prospect of working for eight hours a day.) But this point also applies to involving your kids in public service.

Whether it was soybean forums, the state legislature, serving in Congress, or campaign stops, I took our kids everywhere, and people just got used to seeing them. Yes, we tried to make it fun, with an interesting excursion—and lots of ice cream, which was my favorite, too. And no, not going with me was not an option.

I guarantee our kids got more of a civics education at those "boring" meetings than in their classrooms. And they also got to see how grown-ups interact and try to get things done. As a bonus, they also learned that everything isn't about them, and that every hour doesn't have to be entertaining. The only way I knew how to help them turn out well was to be together as much as possible and bring them along into our world.

Our son, Booker, is amazing in the way he can connect with complete strangers. He can walk into a coffee shop, and if there's somebody sitting alone at a table, in ten minutes they'll be best friends. Did he develop some of those abilities hanging around grown-ups at all those meetings? I'm not sure, but I do know he has a special gift from God to relate to people. Booker has also been in lots of adult conversations, answered phones in the congressional office, given tours of the US Capitol to constituents at the age of eight, and learned that we were there to serve people and care for everyone.

Our culture seems to be growing more and more unfriendly. People don't make eye contact and just keep walking or staring at their phones. I wish more people realized that there is beauty everywhere around them. Stop. Put the phone down and take it in. Thankfully, here in South Dakota, and in many places around the country, people still stop to talk and wave to each other from their cars. But if we want more of this classic American warmth, we must be the ones keeping these traditions alive.

If you're a parent working two jobs, or in a season of life where this sounds impossible, I get it. I really do. I missed many birthdays, sporting events, and activities when I was in Congress, and it still pains me to this day. So, the encouragement is this: take them along as much as you can, and bring them to community meetings, so they can see how civics is done.

Let them hear the debate. Watch the conflict. See the resolution. Know that progress is possible. On the way home, have a conversation about it. And help them apply it to their lives right where they are at.

Everywhere I go, many people have already met or interacted with my children in some capacity, and they always tell me what outstanding people they are: personable, fun, professional, and kind. It makes me so proud. And it's not because Bryon and I preached to them about what to do or not do—although, believe me, we did. But I think it's because they got to see people interact, learn from that interaction, watch their parents handle tough and compassionate situations, and then discuss with them.

Did I screw up sometimes? Absolutely. We talked about that, too. And we still do today. But I think every mistake, every encounter, every conversation was a classroom for my kids, and they benefitted from being a part of my life and my job. Being a parent is hard. Really, really hard. Our job is to give our kids the tools to be successful on their own. We are so proud of how our children have turned out and the lives they lead.

In a way, this commitment to spending time with the people you care about also applies to elected leaders. The more you're with the people you represent, the better job you'll do, and the more "normal" you'll remain.

People don't need elected leaders as much as the elected leaders need the people they serve. And this also holds true when it comes to elections.

VIRGINIA AND THE SILVER BULLETS
Gone are the days when our silent support or even our individual vote is enough to change the direction of our nation. Good candidates need advocates.

We need truth tellers and straight shooters, people who help share accurate information and push back on false information, whether it's in a conversation at church or a post on social media. All the PR firms and ad campaigns in the world are no match for individuals talking openly and honestly to their friends and neighbors about policy, about life. Yes, I know it seems more and more scary to put yourself out there and make the case, but there's really no alternative. And the good news is, once you try it a few times, you'll be pleasantly surprised at the results.

The mob is a tiny percentage of our nation, but they occupy a lot of real estate in the media—especially social media. Our response can be to withdraw from the conversation and keep our views private, which I'm seeing more and more. That's not a winning strategy. Nor is fighting fire with fire by being a bully.

In my view, what really works to change hearts and minds is the same approach I try to use: speak moderately to your friends and neighbors in order to promote conservative values. Think about it: how many lifelong Democrats truly believe our border policy should be to let anyone in and give them free housing, food, healthcare, and a phone as a welcome gift for showing up? No matter how they voted in past elections, do people really want K–12 teachers talking to kids about "gender preference" and more? Our case is not difficult to make. We just need to make it.

The same truth applies to campaigns. After all, we need to elect the right people. I'm always amazed by the people who volunteer at our campaign offices. In 2010, when I was first running for Congress, a group of senior citizens volunteered to help, and wow, they set the bar high. We soon referred to them as Virginia and the Silver Bullets. A dear lady named Virginia was the organizer of the group and made sure everyone knew their job duties and priorities. The group stuffed envelopes, answered phones, and attended every one of my debates. They always sat in the front row because they knew debates made me nervous. I hate to argue with people, and I had never done this before—on a stage anyway. So, they decided to sit in the front row so I could "see faces of people who loved me." It helped me ignore the hate.

I remember many times listening to people shout horrible things at me during a debate, hearing my opponent misrepresent my record, and reading the crazy signs people were waving in the crowd. And then I would look at sweet Virginia's face smiling from the front row, giving me a thumbs-up—and the other Silver Bullets mouthing the words "You're doing great!" It gave me confidence to be strong. There's nothing like support like that when you're in the arena.

If you're thinking about volunteering, here's another tip: bring a friend along. And regardless of how many great ideas (and opinions) you have, try to leave those at the door until you get a better look at how the operations work. As Stephen R. Covey said, "Seek first to understand, then to be understood."[4]

One very wealthy woman and her big-donor friends were instrumental in convincing me to run for Congress. They knew that if I decided to run, I had to win. These ladies took that challenge personally. Yes, they were successful in persuading me. But they didn't just convince me to run. They walked beside me and helped me raise money, which I hate to do. They gave me advice and counsel, but most important, they believed in me and were my friends.

One day I walked into my campaign office and saw this pack leader scrubbing the toilets. I thought, *I bet this lady hasn't cleaned a toilet in years—but look what she is willing to do in order to help.* No job was too humbling or too small for her to tackle. If it needed to be done, she was willing to do it. What an inspiring moment for me.

This experience and many similar moments made me as a candidate even more determined to not disappoint my team. I literally lost sleep thinking about all the people who had invested themselves in our vision. The election was never about me; it was all about the wonderful, generous people around me. And I didn't want to let them down.

Despite appearances, this country isn't powered by social media, pundits, or politicians. It truly runs on power from the people. When we forget that, we go backward. But when we remember and act accordingly, we move forward.

PHOTO OPS OR PEOPLE OPS?

I had the honor of visiting Iowa in January 2024 to support Donald Trump in the caucuses. Not much surprises me about campaigns anymore, but I was really shocked by the number of people I spoke with who support Trump but are scared of making their support public. Of course, there were vocal supporters in Iowa, but many people confessed they were hesitant about caucusing for him and engaging with friends and neighbors.

Even after what I consider an extremely successful four years in office, many are shy about voicing their support, placing signs in their yard, and taking a stand. Maybe it's the classic "Midwest nice" factor and that they don't want to have disagreements with their neighbors, coworkers, or customers. And I get that. Who wants controversy?

The tragedy (yes, *tragedy*) of shrinking back is that we're missing the number one strategy to win elections: people talking with each other with logic and love. I've seen national and state campaigns make the same mistake.

We'll never win the hearts and minds of people if candidates are not interacting with people. The consultants and handlers seem to think the goal of campaign stops are to get great photos and clips for social media. They seem obsessed with creating the *appearance* of momentum than they are about reaching individual voters. Maybe I'm old-school, but it's tough to build enthusiasm online if your ground game is community theater.

I've been in photo-op sessions created by campaign teams that looked impressive online—with six "important" locals shaking hands in strategic locations that were selected to appeal to "regular folks." Makes me want to puke.

If a candidate and those campaigning on their behalf really want to make an impact, they'd have staffers talking to managers of stores and coffee shops asking, "What's your busiest time of the day?"

Let's say it's seven a.m. Then the staffer asks, "Okay, can I have the governor stop in at seven a.m. and meet people? Would you mind putting a sign on your door announcing the date and time? Thanks. We will be posting about the meetup!"

Photo ops are lazy. *People ops* are hard work and a little risky, but effective.

What if two hundred people show up? What if people want to ask questions or shake hands?! Great! Those two hundred people will have a lot to talk about the next few days. And if each one mentions their impressions of the gathering to ten other people, we've reached two thousand people. You never know how what you say to voters in those situations will spark their interest. And you never know what you'll *learn* from people's questions and stories. Yes, it's risky. Yes, there could be hard questions and confrontations. But we will never win hearts and minds if we don't start talking to each other!

Yes, I blame the consultants and the stressed-out staffers for missed opportunities. But the buck stops with the candidate. As the races get bigger, most candidates get farther away from decisions. I stay engaged and hold my staff accountable. I've never lost an election, although some have been close. In January 2024, the Iowa events I participated in on behalf of President Trump exceeded expectations, with over nine hundred people joining me for a rally (while dozens showed up for other candidates' meetings).

The best part of the day was *after* my remarks, when I stepped off the stage greeting people one by one, shaking hands with them and hugging. I took advice and heard stories from people who attended. The consultants call this "working the room." I call it listening. And remembering why I'm there.

UNLIKELY ALLIANCES

Something few people knew about the Mount Rushmore fireworks celebrations on July 3, 2020, which you read about in chapter 7, was just how crucial local support was to the safety and enjoyment of the event.

This was a very controversial public event during the height of COVID, coupled with the fact that the president of the United States would be attending. There are only two main routes to get to Mount Rushmore, but dozens and dozens of small towns and back roads that feed into those routes. From a security standpoint, it's a nightmare. The US Forest Service manages the 1,200-acre national park, but their staff needed additional support. Hundreds if not thousands of Secret Service agents would be there, along with members of the South Dakota National Guard and law enforcement officers from every branch. Even with all these resources, we were concerned about several scenarios.

In one of countless meetings, I said to my public safety secretary, "You know what? These motorcycle guys love Donald

Trump. And we need help to make sure the roads aren't blocked by protesters or troublemakers. There must be a way to engage their help, but the state can't officially request it."

Someone in the room made it clear that they knew what to do, and that was the end of the discussion.

STURGIS SUPER-SPREADERS?

While the July 3 celebration was being planned, another controversial gathering was on the calendar. In August, the annual Sturgis Motorcycle Rally was approaching. Amid the COVID confusion, most people around the country probably assumed we would cancel—the media sure did. But we're not like most people; we give people the opportunity to make their own decisions.

Even when tens of thousands of people marched in the streets of Minneapolis and many other cities, protesting the death of George Floyd, the attention was still on South Dakota's "reckless" decision to host the July 3 celebration and the Sturgis rally. CNN even ran an article with the headline "Over 1,000 Health Professionals Sign a Letter Saying, Don't Shut Down Protests Using Coronavirus Concerns as an Excuse."[5] Other legacy media parroted the same double standard.

Their message was and is "Riots are fine; patriotic gatherings are dangerous."

Our message was, and still is, the opposite: "Come to South Dakota and enjoy some freedom!" In the months approaching the rally, we basically gave the media the collective middle finger, but we did it with a smile and reminded the more than half a million people who would attend to please wash their hands.

Finally, August arrived, and the rally was on. I love to ride motorcycles, but knew if I attended any events or went to any restaurants, it could be a big distraction. That said, I just had to know what was going on and couldn't rely on the media to portray it accurately. The world was going insane during the early months of the pandemic, and I needed to see people enjoy their freedom. I had been speaking about it, defending it, fighting for it—but frankly, I'd been stuck in my office too much and needed a breath of freedom too. So, I jumped in my pickup and took a quick drive out to Sturgis, incognito.

I saw the usual folks enjoying their motorcycles and some normalcy. And I saw some protesters (in masks of course, screaming at the crowd for being so reckless) being politely but firmly escorted out of town by the bikers. I'll say this about the Sturgis crowd: they love America, and they appreciate their freedom. In my drive-by, I saw thousands of Trump flags and bumper stickers. I'm no expert, but I don't think bikers were quite this vocal about politics and candidates before Donald Trump came on the scene. (I've never seen a Romney/Ryan patch on a leather jacket; have you?) Trump emboldened these folks and many others.

BACK TO JULY 3

As the Mount Rushmore celebration drew closer, we believed that all the bases were covered but were still nervous about all the back roads around the area. In an area of hundreds of square miles, it wouldn't take much to shut down a road or important intersection. We couldn't cover every mile of every road. And we couldn't afford to have a small group of trouble-makers block a road and prevent thousands from attending the event. In the back of our minds, we wondered if any bikers would show up to help us.

Boy, did they show up! I heard reports of bikers parked in all the towns along the routes in the Black Hills, and there were license plates from all over the country. Individuals, local motorcycle groups, and even some "motorcycle enthusiasts" offered their own form of peacekeeping. Let's put it this way: if someone wearing a Hell's Angels vest makes it clear they don't have time for any roadblocks, interruptions, or noise, potential disrupters will think twice.

It's also noteworthy that a few months earlier, in May 2020, there was a large Black Lives Matter protest in Sioux Falls, which grew to thousands of people at our local shopping mall. Sparks of violence erupted but never got out of control. There also happened to be hundreds of Second Amendment–loving bikers in close proximity. They parked along the protest route downtown and at the mall, standing with police with their Second Amendment rights on full display. They didn't have to say anything; the message was clear: *no riots or looting tonight.*

I'm not sure what the official statements might be from law enforcement about that night, but I'm sure our police appreciated the additional support. The same folks who appreciate America and appreciate what we were doing to stay free in South Dakota were more than happy to invest time to help. During hundreds of hours of July 3 planning meetings, I kept wondering, *Who else cares about this being a success as much as we do?* The answer is always the same people who love America.

STEP FORWARD

It is not the job of the government to do everything for people. The job of government is to empower people to do things for themselves.

Whether it's an Independence Day celebration, a mayoral campaign, or the safety of your neighborhood, the establishment and the mob are no match for the people. Those who love what America stands for and believe in our future, are a silent majority. But if we stay silent, well, you know what happens.

Send that email.

Make that phone call.

Attend that town hall or homeowners' association meeting.

Volunteer at a campaign. Ask a biker to join you.

If the only voices politicians hear are the consultants and the complainers, we're all in big trouble. Ironically, the people we need most in government are the ones who don't want to be there: moms, dads, college students, farmers, executives, retirees.

You are the most powerful person in government.

○————————○

TWELVE

LEADING FORWARD

My name's Joe Biden. I work for the
government, in the Senate.

<small>—PRESIDENT BIDEN AT A COFFEE SHOP CAMPAIGN STOP, JANUARY 12, 2024[1]</small>

*Whoever would be great among you
must be your servant.*

<small>—MATTHEW 20:26 ESV</small>

T he number one complaint I heard as governor of South Dakota from the business community was they can't find enough employees to fill all the open jobs. Our private and public sectors were growing (and still are), and we needed more skilled workers in every sector to keep moving forward. This problem needed a solution and a strategy.

We had already learned how powerful telling our story was during the pandemic. When the rest of the world shut down, we invited them to come to our state. We knew if people heard about our great way of life, growing economy, and abundance of jobs, many would want to live here. We simply had to get the word out. Our team got to work on a nationwide ad campaign called "Freedom Works Here." We knew there were thousands or even tens of thousands of freedom-loving Americans who wanted to live in a place that honored American values.

We did our research to see what demographics would be most interested and most qualified, who would be open to moving to South Dakota. We identified key states in which to target our efforts. Ads were created for television, digital, and social media. We opened a call center, referred people to businesses, and answered questions about schools, communities, and the weather, of course. The website FreedomWorksHere. com was launched.

Our team mailed follow-up packages and even made some phone calls to people who contacted us. (I enjoyed having several of those conversations myself.)

We started to hear about people who moved to South Dakota simply because of our ads. The mayor of Sioux Falls regularly texted me about new police officers joining their force and all the new people he and his staff were meeting. "Hey, I'm new to South Dakota, and I moved here after seeing those ads and hearing about your state!" People called me from around the state, excited to meet their new neighbors or to finally fill that job with a qualified individual who was so happy to bring their family to where they could finally be free. At the capitol, the team and I had the same amazing experiences of talking with so many new citizens of our great state. Many have stopped by the governor's office to say hello.

Imagine living in a state where people are happy to just be there. That's South Dakota.

The campaign continues, and we're expanding partnerships with businesses and other employers.

We needed nurses, plumbers, electricians, accountants, law enforcement officers, and other professionals. Our ads, in case you haven't seen them, are targeted accordingly, with a funny approach, showing me doing a terrible job at several of these professions. In one ad, I even accidentally shorted out all the lights on the capitol dome because I was such a terrible electrician!

The results have been absolutely fantastic. Our licensing boards are reporting huge increases in people from out of state seeking a South Dakota license, including a 78 percent increase in plumbers, a 44 percent increase in electricians, and a 43 percent increase in accountants. This ad campaign is still young, but we've already seen thousands of families move here, fill our crucial jobs, and create even more jobs, and many more are coming.

Sure, there are those who didn't want our state to change or grow, but the results speak volumes. Businesses expanded, there are more kids in our schools, small towns that were struggling are turning around, and more young people are staying. We're creating a brighter future for everyone in our state.

This is what America was built on. South Dakotans will continue to remind the rest of the country the value of hard work and the dignity it brings. We have the freedom to get up every morning and to provide for ourselves and our families. That's the American dream.

I always say that South Dakotans are some of the hardest-working people I've ever met—no matter how long they've lived here! We still understand the value of hard work. And my goal as governor has never been to create a government that does everything for people, but to create a government that empowers our people to do things for themselves.

Last year, we announced an effort to expand apprenticeship opportunities for professions across the state. We wanted to give workers the opportunity to get trained for a career while still bringing home a paycheck. We wanted to give businesses the support they need to start and expand apprenticeship programs. In just the first two quarters since launching the expanded effort, we've more than doubled the number of new apprenticeships from recent years. And we're just getting started.

I knew that if we could just tell our story, freedom-loving Americans from across the country would want to be a part of what we're doing here. I knew that we needed to celebrate our success, and then take the opportunity to build on it.

That is a story that many people across this country have never heard before. Folks are moving here in record numbers to become a part of our winning way of life. Californians and New Yorkers have never seen a state like ours—one that trusts its people, and one that embraces liberty.

In 2021, when several cities were busy "defunding" police, we began a messaging campaign directed specifically at law enforcement around the country. "If you want to live somewhere people will respect you, come to South Dakota." In the first week almost eight hundred law enforcement officers raised their hands and said "I want to move to South Dakota." When other states and cities were denigrating police and cutting budgets, we were celebrating and welcoming them.

Leaders don't complain; they find solutions and fix stuff.

IT'S TOTALLY FIXABLE, A**HOLE

I'm always looking to develop other leaders—not because I have it all figured out, but because we need more leaders. A few months ago I met with a colleague to offer some guidance on their career. I told the young person, "Honestly, your potential is incredible. You have so many gifts and talents, and your work ethic is off the charts. You work harder than anyone else I know, put in more hours, and are willing to do any job that needs to be done." Then I paused and added, "Problem is, frankly, you're an asshole. Nobody wants to work with you."

The look on his face was a mix of shock and depression. He was listening, so I continued. "You always want to make sure you get the credit for something good that was done, but in the process, you ambush your supervisors and throw others under the bus, and it's just not necessary. We already know you're amazing. I think the world of you. But that's why you are struggling with the team, and why you're missing opportunities for leadership and promotion. Nobody wants to be on your team."

He sunk lower in the chair, like he just received a dismal diagnosis, and stared at the floor. Then I asked, "So . . . do you want to fix it?"

His head popped up. "What do you mean?" he asked.

"This is totally fixable! God gives everybody unique gifts and talents, and we all can learn how to develop them. It's hard to teach people the qualities, intelligence, instincts, and work ethic you already have. The only problem is your attitude and how much you value people. You can fix that. And I'll help you."

Since that conversation, there was an immediate change. And the rest of his team has taken notice. He was always a valuable employee, but now he's becoming a leader.

I believe a big part of my job is to identify and help other leaders—to give them opportunities, insights about their talents, and advice if they want it. It's amazing what just a little bit of encouragement can do to help a leader grow.

HEADS UP, THANK YOU, CELEBRATE

Years ago, as a young rancher, I won a statewide leadership award, and part of the national recognition included a trip to a leadership conference in South Carolina. One of the presenters led a group activity that I'll never forget. I often use it with my team or other groups when I'm speaking on leadership or teamwork. Yes, I know these group activities and ice-breakers can be cringeworthy or make people uncomfortable. But to create better leaders, I have no problem making people uncomfortable for a few minutes in order to get my point across. Here's how it goes.

It starts by having the participants form groups of ten to twelve people each, and asking each group to form a circle with plenty of space between them. The activity leader hands a ball to one of the participants with these instructions for the group.

"We're going to throw this ball to others in the circle, but not the person on either side of you. This ball is your priority. Don't drop it. Take good care of it. Before you throw it to someone, give them a heads-up, like 'Hey Becky, catch!' (By the way, make sure everyone has a few moments to learn each other's names beforehand.) When you catch a ball, say 'Thank you, Matt' before throwing the ball to the next recipient."

It's kind of interesting to see a room full of people tossing a ball around saying "Tom, catch!" "Well, thank you, Tammy. Here, Chuck, ready? Catch!" It's often awkward, having to remind them not to toss to the person next to them, or when someone drops the ball a lot and needs to be reminded to take good care of it. Then we add a few more rules.

"Continue this until everyone in the circle has caught and tossed this ball once. When that is accomplished, find a way to celebrate as group. This can be a cheer, high fives, doing push-ups, or whatever you decide. Celebrate the fact that you accomplished a full circle and then start again. Oh, and don't drop that ball."

As you can imagine, the activity would be simple and fun. The room gets chatty, people start to laugh, they learn each other's names, and we watch their awkward celebrations.

That's when the activity leader quietly hands another ball of a different color to one of the people in the circle. That person often looks at the coordinator with confusion, but the coordinator quickly walks away and moves to the next group to subtly add a ball. The person who just received the new ball invariably decides they better keep things moving, and tosses that ball, following all the same rules.

Things get a bit more complicated at this stage, but the team finds their stride. That's when a third and fourth ball are introduced in the same way, and the fun really starts.

In about five seconds balls are dropping, rolling, and hitting people because there's so much going on. It is chaotic, because people are trying to catch a ball while still having one in their hands, quickly chucking it at someone, or getting hit in the face because there was no warning that someone was throwing them a ball. (Pro tip: use soft foam balls, not golf balls or baseballs.)

After a few minutes of chaos, we take a break to discuss.

"So, what did you learn from that activity?" the leader asks.

"It got so much harder when you gave us more balls to throw and catch."

"What do you mean by *harder*?"

"We dropped a lot of balls and had to run around the room to find them!"

Let the group laugh and tell their stories, then ask, "Well, what happened to the rules. Did you end up breaking any of the rules?"

"Oh yeah, totally. We forgot to say somebody's name before we threw the ball, because we just wanted to be ready for the next one. I forgot to say thank you after catching it. It was impossible to keep track of who touched which colored ball. We didn't know when one ball had made it to everyone in the circle because we had so many balls in the air. And we totally forgot to have a celebration break!

At this point the activity leader asks the crucial question. "At any point during the exercise, did I say you had to throw the second ball around the circle? Or the third or fourth?" The room usually goes dead silent. "I only told you the first ball was your priority—take care of it, and don't drop it. I never said you had to pass the second or third or fourth ball around the circle, did I?"

More silence. But lots of lightbulbs illuminating.

There's so much I love about this activity as it applies to teams and leadership. Let's review.

Just because a project or situation is handed to you, that doesn't necessarily mean it must become the priority of the moment. When people assume this, and when they take their mind off the stated goal, the priority, chaos ensues. And the priority suffers.

When work becomes "busy," we toss responsibilities at each other without communicating ahead of time. And we quickly forget to show gratitude and appreciation for what others are doing.

Most overlooked in these situations is celebration of a goal accomplished. *Who has time to stop and celebrate?!* Effective and healthy teams do.

I'm a driven person, and this has been the toughest lesson for me to remember with the great folks around me who make it all happen. (And by the way, you're still with me here, reading chapter 12. *Thank you!*)

Leaders, remember: heads up, acknowledge people, say thank you, celebrate. And keep track of your priorities, not just problems and questions people throw at you. Success is impossible when you lose your focus the priorities.

IS EVERYONE A LEADER?

There are different kinds of leaders, and we all have various seasons of life. Some "experts" put people into categories of leaders and followers, but I disagree with those labels.

Everyone influences someone, every day, in some way. So, everyone is a leader. If you've been told you're not a leader, consider how much influence you really have with those around you and make a positive difference. And sometimes the best way to influence is to keep your mouth shut.

Probably my best and most pivotal leadership moments happen when I stayed silent and choose to listen to others in the room. Some colleagues told me that when I was in the state legislature, people really paid attention to what I said from the House floor. Was it my eloquent rhetoric? Not exactly. The key was that I rarely spoke, but when I did, it was obvious I had listened to both sides of the argument, done my homework and research, and added insight to the discussion. I didn't repeat other people's points to get some attention. I only spoke when I could add more facts that hadn't been brought up or bring an element to the debate that was missing. Because of this, when I did speak, others listened. And often, my words influenced the outcome.

LEADERS EXAMINE

Leading is not ignoring experts—or ignoring *anyone*. But good leaders thoroughly examine issues themselves before simply relying on others. Then they question the facts and challenge them when needed. Because we all know in this day and age, many people will present opinions or agendas and try to sell them as facts that have nothing to do with reality. This discipline takes time, and you must separate the proverbial wheat from the chaff, but it leads to better conversations and decisions.

When it comes to those you lead, they must know that their perspective is valued and their contributions are considered. Some of the best wisdom I've received was the result of asking my team questions.

I suppose I follow the Russian proverb Ronald Reagan famously quoted to his Soviet counterpart: "trust but verify." And when it comes to crucial matters of accountability within government agencies *(cough, FBI)*, leaders ask questions and examine issues themselves.

I'm often asked by the national media if I think Donald Trump should pick a woman to be vice president. My answer is always about choosing the best people for the job. And I do believe that means intentionally listening to a variety of perspectives—yes, a diversity of backgrounds, experiences, cultures, and opinions, but not in the twisted way the left seeks to define it. We have come too far in this country to simply choose a person to be the vice president of the United States because of their gender, race, or age. We should make sure the best person is chosen.

Remember, it wasn't long ago President Biden's only criteria for picking a United States Supreme Court justice was that the person had to be an African American woman. I'm all for women's rights, but come on, Joe. America deserves the best and most qualified in every case.

LEADERS AND HATERS

My personality tends to ignore affirmation and focus on the one person who might dislike or question me. That sounds a little pathetic, but what I mean is, I could have ten people say really nice things to me and one person criticize me, but the rest of the day, I'll be thinking about the criticism. *Is it true? Even if it's not true, are there a lot of other people who feel the same way?*

Recently, our largest university and my alma mater, South Dakota State University, had the opportunity to play for the college football FCS National Championship in Frisco, Texas, and I wasn't going to miss that game for the world! It was a big moment for this team. I knew many of the young men, and our whole state was so proud of them. (I was also excited to talk some smack in some interviews ahead of the game with the Montana governor, who was there supporting his team.) Of course, we won. *Go, Jacks!* It was their second straight national championship and a great day for every citizen in South Dakota.

During the game, I was introduced to the crowd, and there was plenty of applause and high fives, and I saw many folks wave and yell, "Hi, Kristi!"

But I heard one college kid's voice that stood out: "Hey! Shouldn't you be in South Dakota?!"

For the next ten minutes I tried to focus on the game, all while thinking, *Why would that kid yell that? I'm here supporting our team. Is that wrong? It's a Sunday! What makes somebody do this sort of thing? And wow, he must not like me to yell that across the crowd like that—and I wonder why he felt the need to do that.*

Trust me, this is the mildest form of hatred I deal with on a daily basis. There is much more criticism, ugliness, and just downright awful things said and done that try to affect me on a daily basis. If you can relate, I'll offer what has helped me: continue forward in these situations.

It's difficult to deal with the haters if you have a shred of humanity. It hurts. Accept that fact and be okay with it. Then choose what you really want to be focused on, and who you want to be. Every minute I'm thinking about haters and ugliness, I'm not being grateful, solving problems, or enjoying my day.

The sound of bitter complainers will fade out when we choose life, love, and leadership. And we'll make better decisions.

LEADERS OR LAWYERS?

Leaders are always surrounded by many voices. But when decisions are made, the public's eyes fall on one person: the person who makes the final decision. The press doesn't hound the consultants or the attorneys for accountability. Just because something's legal or done the way it's always been done, that doesn't mean it's right.

Leaders must remember this truth in everything we do. Whether it's the latest virus, threat of war, or political turmoil, you alone are accountable for the choices you make.

We have too much "government by lawyer" in the nation—no offense to attorneys. I have worked with many wise and excellent ones. An exceedingly large percentage of elected officials are lawyers, and one reason for that is because lawmakers should have a solid understanding of the law and how to write laws.

But when you look around at politics today and our "ruling class," do you ever wish we had more lawyers in government? Not me. Recently, we had a situation that required a lot of legal counsel, and even our team of attorneys offered conflicting conclusions.

Trust your gut. Step up. Never appease. Always do what's right—especially when situations are complicated and messy.

LEADERS LEARN FROM HISTORY

As we discussed in chapter 10 on the topic of education, most Americans are dangerously ignorant of our history. This includes many elected officials, sadly.

Understanding of history is a priceless instruction manual. Before calling consultants or attorneys, leaders should ask history: *When did something similar occur? What actions were taken? What was the outcome? What can we learn?*

Every social, political, and military success can be built on wisdom from the past. Just like elected leaders must rely on their oath to the Constitution, we can rely on history to guide decisions.

One of the few times I've not been able to draw relevant historical guidance was during the pandemic. Yes, our nation had experienced similar outbreaks before, but the most recent one was a century old, and our society had changed so much in that time.

As we look forward, are we really living in unprecedented times? Maybe, but I suspect we can always learn from a study of history.

LEADERSHIP IS HORSE SENSE

People are a lot like horses. And if that sounds like an insult to humans, then you don't truly know horses. I've trained a lot of horses and tried to learn all I could about how our different behaviors affect them.

Think about how most people approach horses: they look them straight in the eye, walk directly toward them, and extend their hand to pet their nose, all while talking. These are all the worst things one could do if they want to connect with these amazing animals.

Looking directly at these creatures is taken to be a sign of aggression to horses. Approaching them with squared shoulders is confrontational, and loud voices can be unsettling. An extended hand seems too much like the claws of one of their few natural predators: mountain lions.

If you want to make a new four-legged friend, turn sideways, keep your hands at your sides, look down at the ground, and speak very softly. Then you can slowly yet confidently move a little closer. Once both parties are relaxed, you can even start to take a few steps away from the horse. If some trust has been developed, it will follow. When this happens, the feeling is incredible.

Lots of people, especially in politics, think leadership is being brash and aggressive, tackling situations head-on with a loud voice. This behavior will certainly make people—and horses—move, but not necessarily in the desired direction.

You get the point. Lead by first listening and observing. Then you can go somewhere, and people will follow. Treat them like the precious gifts they are to your leadership journey, and learn from them as well along the way.

PEARLS

One of the things you may notice about me is that I'm always wearing pearls, and people often comment on them. "I like your earrings." "Pretty necklace!" Those conversations open the door for me to tell them about my beautiful friend Shari and why I love pearls.

When I first met her, she told me she had a pearl store, which surprised me. *A whole store filled with jewelry made with pearls?* But then she explained: "Pearls are the only precious gem created by a living creature. In order for the gem to be made, the oyster has to go through something uncomfortable—when a grain of sand gets in the shell. But the oyster endures, and in the end, something precious, beautiful, and unique is created."

Life is hard, uncomfortable, and painful at times. But if we endure, God can use that challenge to make something beautiful out of it, something unique to you and a testimony to His redemptive power and the saving grace He offers each of us.

That's why I always wear something with a pearl, and I pray someone will ask about it so I can share this life-changing story with them.

STEP FORWARD

My brother Robb is someone I'm incredibly proud of. He's run for our local school board multiple times—and lost. But he stays involved because he cares. He doesn't expect others to do what he himself can do. The guy has six kids and a very demanding farming and ranching business. But he was willing to put his name on a local ballot multiple times because he has good ideas. He believes teachers should be paid more and administrators questioned more.

He is a leader who is focused on solutions, not just the problems. We were raised by the same dad, who always said, "Don't complain about things. Fix them!" Dad would be very proud of Robb, too.

My brother Rock is a different kind of leader, one who focuses on individuals and their well-being. He's thoughtful and kind and inquisitive. He never assumes someone is wrong, but that they simply have a different opinion. It's amazing how different my two brothers are, but how necessary their different leadership styles are to our country. We need all approaches to change the hearts and minds of people to move forward.

When it comes to moving our nation forward, we need leaders. But whoa—hold on a second. When you think about leaders, does the next election come to mind?

The next vote is crucial, but what happens—and who happens—before and after the polls close is even more important. Yes, register to vote, and then vote! But if we look to November as the day we move forward, we're deceived.

We need leaders in your community, talking to each other about issues that matter to you. You are the leader we need. You have more influence than any TV ad. No undecided voter ever read a PDF from the RNC and had a dramatic conversion experience. People talking to people about pressing issues is what changes hearts and minds.

What is your vision? What do you want to improve on your street? (Start with fixing a pothole, and believe me, anything's possible from there!) What's wrong with your town, and what are your ideas to help fix it? How can you serve?

Let's have a plan of action for 2024 and beyond. The other side certainly has one.

The leadership problem in this nation is fixable. What are you waiting for?

THIRTEEN

○———————————○

INTO THE FRAY

Once more into the fray
Into the last good fight I will ever know
Live and die on this day

—JOE CARNAHAN, FROM THE FILM *THE GREY*[1]

One of my favorite movies, in addition to *Predator* of course, is *The Grey*. It's no comedy, and not what I'd call family-friendly. (There's a plane crash, lots of hungry wolves, and understandably massive amounts of profanity. No spoilers here though, I promise.) The story fires me up—the constant struggle, determination, and never-give-up attitude of Liam Neeson's character.

One aspect of the film that stays with me is the lines the lead character recites when he finds himself in the worst possible situation. Some might say the words echo lines written by William Shakespeare in *Henry V*. "Once more unto the breach, dear friends, once more."

When I first watched the film, I'd just started in politics, debates, speeches, and policy fights. The words of that poem helped me strengthen my mindset for this new environment I found myself in.

If I screw up, it's over. If I knock it out of the park, I get to live another day.

My worst fear isn't looking dumb or even making mistakes. What I fear most is thinking I could have done more. There's nothing worse than looking back on a situation and thinking, *I wish I would have spoken up, said this or that, or tried harder.*

THE CHAOS AND THE CHOICE

I have a nagging thought: I just hope history remembers me well, that I tried.

To me, the fray means chaos. And the world feels dangerously chaotic right now. I absolutely love that poem because it's a *choice* to enter the fray—and a reminder that every fight could be my last.

My mom will tell you that from the time I was a little girl, every battle I got in was an epic struggle for victory. Surrender was not an option. One time, when I was just a kindergartener, I was lined up with the other kids on the starting line for a foot race.

According to Mom, as the race was about to start, I was hunched over and ready to run alongside all the other students, when I suddenly started sobbing. She rushed over to me to see what the matter was. I looked up at her with tear-filled eyes and cried out "I might lose!" Before the race had even started, the worst thing I could imagine was losing.

That's me—whether it was wearing the shoes I wanted to wear or wearing my brother's jeans because I didn't want to wear girl jeans. And I still don't know how to half-heartedly fight. I always want to win and never want second place. I don't ever want to look back and think, *Maybe I could have done more, fought more, and done better.* Maybe that's because in my head and in my heart, I really do consider that today might be my last day on this earth.

Ever since my dad died unexpectedly when I was twenty-two years old, I was convinced I'd die younger than he did. I don't know why, and I know it doesn't make any sense. But I felt like I was so much like him, and I missed him so much. When someone would say to me, "You're just like your dad," I thought, *Yep. He didn't get much time to do everything he had to do. And I won't either. I'm going to have to move hard and fast to accomplish all I need to.*

Understandably, this attitude has always bugged Bryon and our kids. We can be driving down the road and a hymn will come on the radio, and I'll casually say, "Oh, make sure Aunt Cindy sings that at my funeral."

"*Mom!* Stop it! Quit talking about your funeral!"

Speaking of funerals, several years ago in Wyoming I went to the most amazing funeral of my friend Foster Friess, whom I loved dearly. One of the things that was so special about it was that his casket was brought down the aisle of the church by the Soul Children of Chicago gospel choir. They were dancing and clapping while singing "When the Saints Go Marching In."

The experience was amazing. Celebratory! And I could just see Foster sitting up in heaven, watching the show, and loving it all with his sparkling eyes. He was probably dancing and clapping along. Since then, I've insisted to my family, staff, and friends that my funeral must be like that. "And get that choir to come sing if they will."

I remind them frequently, and they hate it. But to me, it's just going to happen—sooner than we think or want. And I don't dread it. I just need time to get a few more things done!

I've already lived a few more years than my dad did, and in a strange way I feel blessed for every year I've lived beyond that brief span. No one is guaranteed anything. I have a lot more to do if I have any hope of impacting people as much as he did in his lifetime. At his funeral, several people who'd only met him once attended because that one meeting impacted them so much. We still hear new stories about him today, from people we'd never met, how he bought people groceries, paid their utility bills, mentored their kids, showed up to work alongside them when they needed help, and prayed with them when they needed a miracle. He lived every day. And one day he died.

Don't waste a day.

LIVE AND DIE ON THIS DAY

The days I've felt most alive are the days in the fray, fighting for something worthwhile. It could have been working cows, helping my girls at a rodeo, duck hunting with Booker, or fighting on a policy that was good for South Dakota and good for America. Many of my most difficult days are in the fray, and that's living.

How about you? What makes you come alive?

Margaret Thatcher's dad, who was a preacher, offered these words to his hearers and his young daughter: "God wants no faint hearts for his ambassadors. He wants men who having communed with heaven can never be intimidated by the world."[2]

LESSONS LEARNED AND STILL LEARNING

My fellow ambassadors, I'm honored to share these words with you, and I'm honored to stand shoulder to shoulder with you in this fight. In these chapters I've presented lessons learned, and what I'm learning along the way. Here's another look at my encouragement for you.

1. Who's in control? We are, theoretically, but that won't become a reality unless we take back control. When we step into the raging river of politics, we've got to be careful and keep our footing. We need officials who are focused on their oath to the Constitution.

2. Campaigns are weird and tough, but it's part of keeping a republic. Your involvement really matters. Don't let any elected official or government "expert" talk down to you. It really isn't that complicated. Trust your gut.

3. We need people who break what's broken. But we need builders even more—at every level of government and in our communities. True builders don't think they're better than anyone else.

4. When the difference between right and wrong is clear, there's no room for compromise or passing the buck. As you step into the arena and talk with elected officials, remember that your voice matters, despite what the establishment wants you to believe. If you're an elected official or running for office, remember to speak moderately— with forethought—to make your case.

5. The next crisis is always around the corner. Panic is not an excuse to abandon our laws or our Constitution. It's in challenging times that our values and convictions are put to the test. Be ready. Be loyal to what matters.

6. The entire world is watching the United States of America. We need leaders who have a solid understanding of life outside our nation but are clear that our nation is always the number one priority. And we need people like you to help elect them.

7. Ignore the doubters—including your own doubts. Form a wolf pack. You and your friends can support each other and kick some butt.

8. Cultural decline is not inevitable. There really are forces at work trying to erode our values and freedoms. Live your beliefs, and let your actions speak. Then, when you're ready to make your case, you can persuade others.

9. Losing sucks. Winning is better. Get to know your state's secretary of state, and make sure your election rules and systems are solid. When it comes to turning donkeys into elephants in the next election, I can't imagine a better time to make our case, based on a shared love for our country.

10. For our children's sake, and for the sake of their education, we can't trust the government to do what's best for our kids. We've seen what happens when we naively expect them to honor our historical values. You know what to do.

11. The political soap opera that is Washington, DC, is captivating—and deceptive. You are the most powerful person in government. What's decided in your homeowner's association meetings, town hall, county commissioner's meetings, or state capitol is just as important—and often more important—than what makes national headlines. What happens locally will happen nationally. The more we exercise our freedom of speech, the more difficult it will be to have others try to silence us.

12. We need leaders. And we need leaders who raise up more leaders. Everyone is a leader because everyone influences. Leaders remember to give people a heads-up, thank them, and take time to celebrate. Leaders keep their eye on the ball and keep their priorities straight.

Remember, help is on the way, and *you* are that help.

BE "SOMEONE" OR DO SOMETHING?

United States Air Force fighter pilot Colonel John Boyd was an influential figure in his military career, which began in the 1950s. His innovative strategies have not only been applied to aerial combat—where they are still taught—but in business, leadership, and legal circles. His "to be or to do" speech applies to our fight today:

> You're going to have to make a decision about which direction you want to go. If you go that way you can *be somebody.* You will have to make compromises and you will have to turn your back on your friends. But you will be a member of the club and you will get promoted and you will get good assignments.
>
> Or you can go that way and you can *do something*—something for your country and for your Air Force and for yourself. If you decide you want to do something, you may not get promoted and you may not get the good assignments and you certainly will not be a favorite of your superiors. But you won't have to compromise yourself.
>
> You will be true to your friends and to yourself. And your work might make a difference.

To be somebody or to do something. In life there is often a roll call. That's when you will have to make a decision.

To be or to do? Which way will you go?[3]

As we know, there are plenty of people who get into politics to "be somebody." They compromise and seem to get all the good "assignments." And they always turn their backs on us when they get into power.

No more. No going back.

STEP FORWARD

Brace yourself, whether you're a member of Congress or going to your first school board meeting. Let's dispense with "live to fight another day." Let's hate compromise as much as we hate defeat.

I've got steel in my veins now that I'm a grandma. Something amazing happens when you become a grandma: you're sad when you can't be with them and amazed at how brilliant and smart they are when you're together.

I want them to live in a strong, free country. But no, it's much more than that. I must do everything I can to leave our state and nation better than I found it. I will fight for them and give my all.

Perhaps America will decline. Someday. But not on my watch.

Let's go, once more into the fray.

FOURTEEN

DAY ONE

> This is about deciding who is ready for day one to unite
> this country and demonstrate that they could.
>
> —PRESIDENTIAL CANDIDATE JOE BIDEN, NOVEMBER 2019[1]

> *[Interviewer] says, "You're not going to be a dictator, are*
> *you?" I said, "No, no, no. Other than day one." We're*
> *closing the border, and we're drilling, drilling, drilling.*
> *After that, I'm not a dictator.*
>
> —DONALD TRUMP, DECEMBER 2023 INTERVIEW[2]

I t wasn't always this way, but presidential candidates seem to talk a lot about what they'd do in office on day one.

In 2017, in his first full day in office, President Trump signed an executive order to move toward the repeal of the Affordable Care Act, and he froze new federal regulations.[3]

President Biden had a busy first day.[4]

He issued a "100 Days Masking Challenge" and asked Americans to do "patriotic duty" and mask up for one hundred days. Then he reengaged with the World Health Organization "to Make Americans and the World Safer." Biden extended "Eviction and Foreclosure Moratoriums," enacted a "Student Loan Pause," and rejoined the Paris Agreement on climate change.

After changing pens, he went on to launch a "Whole-of-Government Initiative to Advance Racial Equity" and reversed President Trump's executive order "Excluding Undocumented Immigrants from the Reapportionment Count" so illegal immigrants would be counted in the census.

But wait—there's more! President Biden reversed the so-called Muslim ban and stopped construction of the wall at the southern border. #Visionary #Sarcasm

And in perhaps his most ironic move, he ordered every appointee in the executive branch to sign an ethics pledge. Not sure if Hunter was considered an appointee, and it's unclear if Biden signed the pledge himself.

Soon after day one, he canceled the Keystone XL Pipeline.

BOY, WOULD I DO THINGS DIFFERENTLY FROM BIDEN

What would I do if I was president on the first day in office in 2025? Thanks for asking. I happen to have a list.

The first thing I'd do is make sure Joe Biden's dog was nowhere on the grounds ("Commander, say hello to Cricket for me"). But my dog, Foster, would sure be welcome. He comes with me to the capitol all the time and loves everyone.

Close the border.

Restore building the Keystone XL Pipeline to fuel up our energy infrastructure.

I would have ice cream for everyone, and this policy would stay in effect.

Build that wall and restore the "remain in Mexico" policy.

Hire John Kerry as climate czar just to have the satisfaction of looking him in the eye and saying, "You're fired!"

Open up more land for oil and natural gas exploration.

Schedule a bake sale to raise money for Alexandria Ocasio-Cortez, Elizabeth Warren, and any other members of Congress who think they're underpaid.

Put a bunch of federal property up for sale. You would not believe how many empty government buildings there are, and the millions of dollars it takes to maintain them.

Take the Beast out for a spin, see what it could really do. *Would they let me drive it? Wait, I'd be the president, of course they would let me drive it . . . right?*

Order the construction of a corral on White House grounds, so I could take my horses Ice Man and Blondie for rides whenever I needed a break.

Invite a bunch of Republicans—and Democrats—to the White House to start working on an actual immigration policy. And, if they didn't want to solve the problem, I'd do what I could via executive orders. Protecting the people of the United States would be my top job, and I wouldn't allow politics to get in the way of our security.

Move federal agencies out of Washington, DC, and into states where normal people live, so they can talk with those who actually have to deal with their policies and programs.

Require all members of Congress to drive a twenty-year-old Buick LeSabre. Dents optional.

Mandatory five a.m. daily workout for all members of Congress.

Figure out what the heck the United Nations actually does for us and why we send them billions to work against

American interests and values. Then, I would make sure we don't send them another dime until every other nation pays their fair share. Same with NATO countries.

Invite the Obamas and Bidens over to watch *The Grey*. (We'd make it a matinee, for Joe.)

Sign a "Declaration of Common Sense" (also known as the "'Duh' Proclamation")

1. A man is a man. A woman is a woman. #TrustTheScience

2. Men should not use women's bathrooms or compete in women's sporting events. Ever.

3. One person, one vote.

4. Elections are more easily tampered with when we rely upon mail-in ballots and touchscreens.

5. Illegal immigration is . . . illegal.

6. Farmers and ranchers and all the people who grow and prepare our food deserve more honor than celebrities, politicians, and bureaucrats.

7. "Gender-affirming care" for minors is child abuse.

8. Nobody gets smarter or more motivated by using dope.

9. Guns are not the problem. Criminals are.

10. Racial discrimination is always wrong. Racial prefer-
    ences and quotas are discrimination. Diversity,
    equity, and inclusion is racism.

11. Diversity of opinion and perspective can be valuable.
    But actual strength comes from unity.

12. Environmental, social, and governance policies
    destroys companies and countries. Most of all, it
    hurts investors and normal Americans, while enrich-
    ing a ruling class.

13. Teachers report to parents, not the other way around.

14. "Strongly worded" letters from representatives in
    Congress aren't worth the paper they're printed on.
    (Find a way to actually effect positive change.)

15. Free speech is sacred (including speech you might not
    like).

16. The United States should grow our own food, make
    our own medicines, produce our own energy, and be
    as self-sufficient as possible. When we do need to buy
    stuff from other countries, buy only from our allies.
    No exceptions.

17. Kids need to learn about history and civics, and they
    need to understand why it's important.

18. Leverage oil and natural gas to power our technological advances in energy.

19. If you take out a student loan, pay it back. That's how this works.

20. All this nice stuff comes from capitalism, not socialism.

21. Elections are not a threat to democracy.

22. You are the most important person in government, not any elected official. Your voice matters more than the establishment wants you to realize.

In your heart, you know I'm right.

I'm sure there are things missing, but that's what day two is for.

STEP FORWARD

What would *you* do on day one as president of the United States?

Be a forward thinker, because there is no going back.

THE STATE OF FREEDOM

Adapted from my 2023 budget speech

The last four years, we have made South Dakota the strongest state in America.

We lead the nation in almost every single economic metric. Our personal income growth is number one. And over the last year, both our new housing development and new business applications have been the best in America. Our kids lead the nation in educational outcomes, and we are breaking tourism records year after year.

This past year, our unemployment rate has been the lowest it's ever been in history. Today, we have fewer than seven hundred people in the entire state on unemployment.

I recognize that taxpayer dollars are not our own—they belong to the people of South Dakota. We all must remember throughout our budget discussions, that this money belongs to the hardworking people of South Dakota.

In South Dakota, our state motto declares "Under God the people rule." These aren't just words we say— we believe them and take action based on them. We *must* for the future security of our great state.

Frankly, the irresponsibility of the federal government demands it. No nation in history has ever survived the tax burden and spending spree that this White House is pursuing. They haven't balanced the federal budget in decades, Congress continues to raise the debt limit with no plan for spending, and leaders in DC print money only to turn around and go in debt to foreign entities that are our enemies.

Then they declare that they *must* reach into the pockets of everyday Americans to grab more of their earnings to keep us safe, enforce law and order, and subsidize programs designed to enslave families to the government. We have seen the incredible power grab of these leaders the past few years. They have used unconstitutional actions and the enticement of more money to take unprecedented action to make people more dependent, weak, and apathetic. It is irresponsible and wrong.

That's not how we run our state. We make hard decisions and recognize that a limited government respects people *and* their dollars, and that it is the way to preserve the American dream for our children and our grandchildren. We don't make decisions to only benefit us today.

We look far into the future and realize the ramifications of our decisions and make the hard choices, so that future South Dakotans have the chance to grow up in a place of opportunity and freedom.

The nation is watching how we, as leaders, make decisions. Since 2020, Americans now know where South Dakota is—on the map and on issues of freedom. They see this state as a beacon of hope. A place of liberty. How we decide to govern, budget, and communicate to our people will be watched, evaluated and judged. Has my job gotten easier with more revenue? I would say no. It is much harder.

We must be disciplined in order to protect our state from an expansion of government in our lives through new programs and subsidies. Let's not forget that the government should be beholden to the people and not the other way around. Our Founding Fathers did not believe in a centralized government. They believed in the rights of individuals and their ability to govern themselves.

People are making more money, our businesses have expanded, we have recruited new industries, and because of the way we have followed our states' motto "Under God the people rule," we have permanently grown the state's economy. We have lived through unprecedented challenges since I've been governor: bomb cyclones, tornadoes, flooding, a pandemic, the derecho—but make no mistake, this economic growth is an unprecedented event as well. We must be leaders who protect South Dakota's way of life as we look to the future.

On November 8, 2022, the people of this great state gave us a mandate. They turned out in record-breaking numbers to make sure we heard from them loud and clear. They demand low taxes. Less regulation and more freedom. They were also clear that they want us to take care of people and create opportunities to succeed. As governor, I will continue to listen to our people. I will guide our discussion and decisions based on my constitutional authority.

We have hundreds of millions of dollars in our state's reserves and trust accounts. Historically, our goal is to keep 10 percent of our annual budget in these funds. Since I've been governor, we have almost doubled that number.

We ended last year with a record-breaking budget surplus of $115.5 million.

That historic surplus in fiscal year 2022 was largely thanks to sales and use tax receipts growing by more than 12 percent over the prior fiscal year. In fiscal year 2023, sales and use taxes have grown by another 14.1 percent. In South Dakota we know to prepare for the future.

We have done everything we can in our state to be successful; however, economists indicate there will be challenges ahead. Bad policies coming out of Washington, DC, will unleash a recession in this country. Like it or not, we will be impacted. Earlier this year our country had two consecutive quarters of negative economic growth. The Federal Reserve's increase of interest rates is another indicator that a recession is on the horizon.

But South Dakota's growth in tax revenues continued, because our state's economy is in a far stronger

position than the nation's as a whole. Economists
expect that the upcoming recession will be primarily
investment led. They expect that our unemployment
rate will remain low. And they don't expect consumer
spending to be heavily impacted. Those factors affect
how we budget here in our state.

In my budget, I am keeping our revenue projec-
tions for the future very conservative. The people of
South Dakota deserve safe planning that protects
them from future tax increases or drastic cuts to state
services.

Eliminating the sales tax on groceries is the biggest way that my budget could help South Dakotans
tackle the challenge of Biden's inflation and protect
hard-earned money. Unfortunately, food costs have
risen by far too much. And families are struggling to
make ends meet as a result.

I have worked hard to educate leaders about how
the rapid increase of the costs of milk, ground beef,
eggs, and other groceries affects everyday families in
our state.

Eggs alone have increased to over 140 percent of
what they were a year ago. Even with South Dakota
having the best personal income growth, family budgets are not keeping up. We can grow incomes even
more by letting people keep more of their own hard-
earned money in their pockets.

Gas prices continue to increase because of President
Biden's energy policies. New regulations and taxes, a
lack of utilization of American energy sources, and a
dwindling reserve indicate this trend will continue.

Senior citizens, working parents, single moms—
every South Dakotan is paying more for food, for gas,
and to heat and cool their homes. Their family
finances are struggling under the strain. Over the last
ten years, Americans have saved 7 to 8 percent of their
monthly income on average.

During the pandemic, that jumped to 20 to 30
percent. Today, they are saving less than 4 percent
because almost every dollar they make is needed to
pay their monthly bills. They are no longer saving for
college or to buy a new house or a new car. They are
just barely getting by. We need to give them relief, and
we can do so by giving them a tax cut by eliminating
the sales tax on groceries.

The state legislature was not in favor of cutting
taxes. The Senate was clear at the beginning of session
that there would be no cut in taxes that would pass.
The House seemed more willing to have a debate, so I
proposed what I believed would be the best fiscal tax
policy to benefit our citizens, especially in light of the
hyperinflation they were seeing in food costs and the
overall health of our state revenues.

But letting the people keep more of their own
hard-earned money always makes politicians uneasy.

Unfortunately, the state legislature chose to go
with a temporary reduction in the overall sales tax
rate of 4.5 percent to 4.2 percent for the next four
years, instead of repealing the sales tax on groceries.
That type of tax holiday will benefit those who visit
our state, is not targeted toward our citizens, and will
only be in place for a short period of time. It will allow

taxes to rise again and create less certainty for families here at home. I disagreed with this approach to cutting taxes but signed the budget with it included so families could receive some relief; they overwhelmingly wanted a tax cut, although they preferred a permanent tax cut on groceries.

Remember, our revenues are strong because we have grown our economy and it is the strongest in the nation. People have moved their families, their jobs, and their businesses to South Dakota. Our new housing developments are here to stay. New industries are thriving. The jobs of the future are right here in South Dakota. And once again, we have the fastest growing incomes in America.

This growth is *sustainable*—and available to every citizen of every state.

APPENDIX B

FREEDOM WORKS HERE

Adapted from my 2024 State of the State address[1]
January 9, 2024

W e are in a different time than we were just five short years ago.

We used to talk about what we believe as conservatives and the importance of limited government, low taxes, American values, and personal responsibility. But then challenging times hit our state, our country, and our world. And we had to decide just how conservative we really were going to be here in South Dakota. Were we just going to talk about limited government and freedom, or fight for it—defend it?

Even when it wasn't the popular thing to do, we stood strong on the Constitution and our state's motto: "Under God the people rule."

South Dakota is doing better than every other state in the nation because we have embraced conservative principles. I've often called our state small, more like a pilot project for conservative reforms to prove if they really do work. And we have proven that

231

they do. Our people are thriving, our economy is growing, and the state has never been in a more stable fiscal situation. We have cut taxes, created jobs, and maximized opportunities. We have also learned that there is a trick to keeping that momentum going. We have learned that we have to tell our story in order to succeed.

We can govern conservatively, but we also need to keep our foot on the gas. South Dakota's success is unprecedented. And we have a limited window of time when the eyes of the entire nation are on our state. We cannot miss the opportunity to capitalize on that.

During my second inaugural address last year, I gave a top ten list of things that surprised me about being governor. Well, I think it's time for another such list. I can't possibly cover today for all of you all of the wonderful things that we are doing in our state. But I can hit the highlights.

I am proud to present my top ten list of things we are doing here in South Dakota to ensure that freedom works here.

#10: FREEDOM TO KEEP AND BEAR ARMS

We protect our Second Amendment rights. Constitutional carry was the very first bill that I signed into law. Two years ago, you all worked with me to make our state the first in the nation to waive all fees for concealed carry permits. We even pay for people's federal background checks. It doesn't cost South Dakotans a penny to exercise their Second Amendment rights.

And last year, I signed an executive order that says that the state will not do business with any financial institution who infringes on people's Second Amendment rights.

We have been able to market our state as a Second Amendment haven. My Office of Economic Development is actively working to recruit firearms businesses from states that infringe on the Second Amendment to move here. Last year, California became the first state in America to levy a special tax on guns and ammunition, and we immediately invited California gun manufacturers to move here to South Dakota.

We've proven that freedom works for these gun manufacturers. They're moving here, growing, and thriving. Cole-TAC in Rapid City and Silencer Central in Sioux Falls have both had leadership who moved to South Dakota for a better life. These folks built thriving companies that employ South Dakotans and help our people exercise their Second Amendment rights. Other companies like H-S Precision, Black Hills Ammunition, and TS Custom Precision Rifles are a big part of helping this industry grow in South Dakota. Many of the leaders of these firearms businesses here with us today, would you all please stand? Thank you for giving South Dakotans the opportunity to utilize their Second Amendment rights!

And we aren't going to stop there. Just last month, our Department of Game, Fish, and Parks began moving dirt for a world-class shooting range West River. The South Dakota Shooting Sports Complex will be the premier firearms range in the Midwest. But the Biden administration is undermining this project by changing the rules after they had already signed off. I am working with the Department of Game, Fish, and Parks to continue to build this range which will host world class events here in South Dakota and impact our economy long term.

#9: FREEDOM TO ENJOY THE OUTDOORS

My administration has made it a priority to enhance our outdoors opportunities. Every year, we're ranked either number one or number two for the most hunting licenses per capita. My Second Century Initiative is expanding opportunities for animal habitat across the state. South Dakota has more than 5 million acres of public access hunting opportunities, even though 80 percent of our land is privately owned. In 2023, we broke the record for most private land enrolled into public hunting access. The reason why is very simple: respect. We respect each other's private property rights and seek permission to hunt on our neighbors' land before we set foot on the property.

My Nest Predator Bounty Program is aimed at teaching respect for the outdoors and wildlife to our kids and grandkids. Every year, participants turn in fifty thousand tails of predators that would otherwise devastate our pheasant and wildlife population. This past year, 46 percent of the program's participants were under the age of eighteen, and that number has been steadily increasing every year. We're getting more South Dakota kids involved in trapping, fishing, and hunting.

#8: FREEDOM TO FARM AND RANCH

Hunting is fundamental to South Dakota's way of life, but I can think of one thing that's even more fundamental: farming. We're in the top ten in the country for production of about twenty-five different agricultural commodities. Our farmers and ranchers provide about 30 percent of our state's economic output. South Dakota farmers are free to farm; South Dakota ranchers are free to ranch.

Last year, I brought forward legislation that would have stopped foreign adversaries from purchasing ag land in South Dakota. China and other evil foreign governments are executing a plan to own our land and control our food supply. Although last year's proposal to regulate these purchases did not pass, we have continued to discuss solutions. Congress has not taken action, and we cannot afford to wait another year. In just the past decade, China's ownership of American ag land has increased by 5,300 percent. This is far too important to our national security to let another year go by and let our enemies gain a larger foothold in our economy and food supply chain. South Dakota respects the freedom to farm and ranch. That freedom should not extend to our enemies.

#7: FREEDOM TO BE SECURE

One of the biggest reasons that we cannot allow America's adversaries, like China, to own South Dakota ag land is because Ellsworth Air Force Base is going to soon be the first home of the next-generation bomber that will keep America safe for decades to

come. The B-21 Raider took its first test flight just two
months ago. And our enemies are going to do everything in their power to get intelligence on that bomber.
It is our duty to do what we must to ensure that they
fail—and that we succeed at keeping our people safe.

Sometimes, keeping our people safe means that
we need to extend our efforts beyond South Dakota.
The Biden administration's failures at the border have
been so well documented that I don't need to go into
them at great length here. For the third time in less
than three years, South Dakota National Guard
troops went to help. When I was with our soldiers at
the border, I saw the inhumanity of Biden's failed
policies.

Until those policies change, the lack of security at
the southern border is making South Dakotans less
safe here at home. Drugs and human trafficking are
devastating communities. More than 70 percent of the
overdose deaths in America are now caused by fentanyl. South Dakota is not immune. We have led the
nation in the decrease in overdose deaths two out of
the past three years, and we are second lowest in the
nation overall. But we can't stop there—we need to
tackle the rising challenge of fentanyl and address the
drug xylazine, otherwise known as the "zombie"
drug.

#6: FREEDOM TO GET A SECOND CHANCE

But if South Dakotans do get involved in drugs or
another aspect of crime, that should not be the final
word. Their punishment should match their crime,

but they should also have the opportunity to rehabilitate and become better, more capable members of our society.

The new prisons that we are working together to construct will help achieve this, but we are not waiting until they are constructed to provide second chances for our people. Late last year, I spoke at a graduation for the Sixth Circuit Problem-Solving Court. Eight graduates—all of whom had been sober for a year or more—stood up and shared their stories and their hopes and dreams for the future. In fact, more than 150 South Dakotans graduated from this initiative last year. This is a rigorous program that includes five phases and requires frequent alcohol and drug testing. It's a proven strategy that reduces recidivism, saves taxpayer dollars in the long run, and restores hope and dignity for these individuals.

Last month, I commuted the sentence of a number of inmates who qualified, giving them parole. They had been incarcerated with ingestion as their highest offense. Now they can begin their supervised transitions back into the community. We will continue to evaluate these second-chance opportunities for those who can prove they deserve them.

Once individuals are out of custody and back into society, we want them to have the opportunity to build a career so that they can provide for themselves and their families. In the last several years, we have advanced licensure reform in a variety of ways. There is another step on this path that we should take. My Department of Labor and Regulation is bringing legislation to provide second-chance license opportunities. This bill creates a set of standards to consider criminal histories and any possible rehabilitation by applicants and licensees. We need more plumbers, more electricians, and more welders, and an unrelated criminal past shouldn't stop qualified applicants from filling these roles.

#5: FREEDOM TO BE RESPECTED

Providing these kinds of opportunities is about dignity—and it's also about respect. We should respect every person as an individual, as an equal, as an American. Tomorrow, on State Tribal Relations Day, we will advance an effort that I have been working on since I became governor. We will hang tribal flags in the rotunda of this capitol. Three years ago, I signed legislation allowing our state's nine Native American tribes to have their respective tribal flags hung in the rotunda. We will hang the first of those flags: the flags of the Standing Rock Sioux Tribe and the Rosebud Sioux Tribe. Our tribes are part of who we are as South Dakotans, and we will respect their heritage.

We will also continue to support the freedom of our Jewish and Israeli neighbors to be respected. On October 7, Hamas terrorists committed atrocities against the nation of Israel, some of which are so savage they are unspeakable. Since then, further hate and discrimination has occurred in America at an increased rate of 388 percent over the last year. College campuses across the country have become breeding grounds for disgusting antisemitic acts. The more it happens, the more it will be normalized. We must stop it before that happens. I am proud to support legislation this year to define antisemitism to make it easier to prove when conduct is motivated by antisemitism. This strengthens our antidiscrimination laws and ensures our allies and our citizens are safe and protected.

#4: FREEDOM TO LEARN

This includes supporting the teachers who give our kids that opportunity to learn. Teachers' salaries have not kept up with increased funding to education. After this year, we will have raised funding to K–12 in South Dakota by more than 26 percent since I have been governor, but teacher pay lags far behind. Our teachers deserve better.

Yes, I know that schools have their own challenges. But I also know this: the Blue Ribbon recommendation wasn't just that teacher pay would go up—the Blue Ribbon promise was that teachers would be the first priority—that they would be paid more. So let's do it.

In my budget address last month, I discussed the particular success of the Jobs for America's Graduates program, which is preparing at-risk high school students for college or a career once they graduate.

When students graduate, we want them to have every opportunity open for them. Some of them will jump right into a career—and that's great! Some of them will go to one of our tech colleges—and we have some of the very best in the nation. Some will go to college. Some might even join our National Guard and then go to college. The young adults who make that brave choice to raise their right hand and serve our nation deserve our utmost respect, our thanks, and our support. Last year, this body worked with me to extend tuition for South Dakota National Guardsmen and Guardswomen to 100 percent at our state universities. I'm asking you to finish the job and extend that opportunity to soldiers and airmen who choose to go to private colleges here in South Dakota.

#3: FREEDOM TO BE HEALTHY

In South Dakota, we value living a healthy life, no matter where you live. Every South Dakotan should have the freedom to live where they want—but they shouldn't have to choose between a rural way of life and good health outcomes. In our rural communities, emergency responders are sometimes the only local healthcare providers. They often show up in our very worst moments. But the nationwide EMT turnover rate is 36 percent. And in South Dakota, nearly 90 percent of our emergency medical services are done by volunteers.

I have worked to support the dedicated men and women of this critical workforce. For the past two years, my Department of Health has been working to advance EMS access across our state with a $20 million investment.

One of the first major calls to Telemedicine in Motion came last December. A rancher was out caring for his buffalo when he was attacked by one of his animals. His injuries were life threatening—dozens of injuries from the horns and hooves of the animal, multiple broken ribs, lungs filling with blood, broken neck, and more. After pulling himself into a front-loader and driving back home for help, he was picked up by the local EMS agency who connected with the Avel team via telemedicine. A board-certified physician and nurses were on camera to help stabilize the rancher, coordinate with the receiving hospital, and activate the care flight team to expedite the transfer of the patient to Sioux Falls. Once the EMS crew arrived at the hospital, Avel maintained their support of the patient since Avel Emergency was installed in the hospital's ER. After the patient recovered, he shared feedback with the care team: "They held my life in their hands and gave it back to me, something that I will be forever grateful for."

These efforts are an investment in the future of EMS. More importantly, they are saving lives.

#2: FREEDOM FOR LIFE

In order to live a healthy life, we must first have the freedom get off to the right start. That freedom extends to every single South Dakotan—before they are born, after they are born, and until the day they die. Later this week, I will proclaim that 2024 will be "Freedom for Life Year" in South Dakota. The most important way that we will advance this is by taking care of both moms and their babies before birth *and* after. Being pro-life means valuing the child's life before their birth and throughout their life; it also means valuing and protecting that mother's life.

The first thousand days of a child's life (from the moment they are conceived to their second birthday) are the most significant days for their development. Research in the fields of neuroscience, biology, and early childhood development has given us powerful insights into how nutrition, relationships, behaviors, and environments in the first thousand days shape future outcomes. Mom and baby must be both well nourished and cared for—that will lead to healthy physical, emotional, and mental growth as a child's brain and body grow and develop. For instance, poor nutrition in the first thousand days can cause irreversible damage to a child's growing brain, affecting their future in school and beyond. It can also set the stage for later obesity, diabetes, and other chronic health problems. It can even contribute to the next generation's risk of poverty and poor health and behavioral outcomes.

If a baby is exposed to drug use, alcohol or tobacco use, poor health environments, or sexually transmitted illnesses; if there is a lack of good hygiene in the home or lack of prenatal care and well child visits; if the child's mother is abused; if the child does not have a safe sleep environment—each of these can have countless negative impacts on that baby's future.

We care about the lives of our mothers and children. We have dedicated resources and time. But we can still do more to prevent the rising death rates of South Dakota moms and babies, particularly among Native Americans living on tribal lands.

So what are we doing in South Dakota? We are offering the Bright Start program to get one-on-one nursing services to first-time moms and their babies from pregnancy until the child's second birthday. The Department of Social Services' Pregnancy Health Home will offer care coordination to all pregnant mothers who are enrolled in Medicaid. These moms also have access to prenatal and postpartum coverage for up to a year after birth along with well-child and health maintenance exams.

The majority of infant deaths can be directly tied to unsafe sleep habits, so DOH provides safe sleep recommendations and education to new and expecting parents.

We help moms and families that struggle with smoking, drugs, or alcohol. The Department of Social Services provides help for pregnant moms struggling with substance abuse disorder, walking with them and holding them accountable through their treatment.

We are doing all of this and so much more to help moms, families, and their babies both before birth and after. You can find all of this information in one place on Life.SD.gov. Moms can go there to answer questions about pregnancy, parenting, available financial resources, adoption, and more.

#1: FREEDOM TO WORK

This is what America was built on. South Dakotans will continue to remind the rest of the country the value of hard work and the dignity it brings. We have the freedom to get up every morning and to provide for ourselves and our families. That's the American dream.

I always say that South Dakotans are some of the hardest-working people that I have ever met. We still understand the value of hard work. And my goal as governor has never been to create a government that does everything for people, but to create a government that empowers our people to do things for themselves.

When a global pandemic hit, many states closed down. South Dakotans kept working. While other states were experiencing record high unemployment levels, we broke the national record for the lowest state unemployment less than a year ago. We are creating opportunities for people to get into the career of their dreams. Last year, we announced an effort to expand apprenticeship opportunities for professions across the state. We wanted to give workers the opportunity to get trained for a career while still bringing home a paycheck. We wanted to give businesses the support they need to start and expand apprenticeship programs. In just the first two quarters since launching the expanded effort, we've more than doubled the number of new apprenticeships from recent years.

We are continuing the Freedom Works Here workforce recruitment campaign. This campaign is only six months old, and we've received thousands of applicants interested in moving to our state just through the program, not counting those who independently made the move. Thousands have already moved here! The ads have been viewed about 850 million times nationwide.

These ads are so successful because they tell South Dakota's story. Our state licensing boards are reporting huge increases of out-of-state applicants seeking licenses in South Dakota—including a 78 percent increase in plumbers, a 44 percent increase in electricians, and a 43 percent increase in accountants. Our labor force has grown by more than ten thousand people in just the last year. Our license recognition bill combined with the microphone of Freedom Works Here is a powerful tandem to fill these much-needed jobs.

That is a story that many people across this country have never heard before. Folks are moving here in record numbers to become a part of our winning way of life.

NOTES

INTRODUCTION: HELP IS NOT ON THE WAY

1 "Transcript: Mayor Adams Appears on WABC-TV's Tiempo," City of New York, December 17, 2023, https://www.nyc.gov/office-of-the-mayor/news/971-23/transcript-mayor-adams-appears-wabc-tv-s-tiempo.

2 Kristine Parks, "NYC Protester Slams Dems' Response to Migrant Crisis: 'Destroyed Our City,'" Fox News, September 15, 2023, https://www.foxnews.com/media/nyc-protester-slams-dems-response-migrant-crisis-destroyed-our-city.

3 Matthew Brown, David Jackson, and Maureen Groppe, "Protesters outside the White House Make Themselves Heard Inside as Trump Delivers RNC Speech," *USA Today*, August 28, 2020, https://www.usatoday.com/story/news/politics/elections/2020/08/27/rnc-protesters-white-house-trump-acceptance-speech/5652010002.

CHAPTER 1: WHO'S IN CONTROL?

1 Derek Cheng, "Coronavirus: Jacinda Ardern Dismisses Nationwide Lockdown Speculation on Social Media," *New Zealand Herald*, March 18, 2020, https://www.nzherald.co.nz/nz/coronavirus-jacinda-ardern-dismisses-nationwide-lockdown-speculation-on-social-media/I2FTKPSA36LJIDNLBFIYECXDHM.

CHAPTER 2: CONGRESS, CAMPAIGNS, AND CASH

1 John McTiernan, director, *Predator*, 1987.

2 Dwight D. Eisenhower Presidential Library, "Quotes," https://www.eisenhowerlibrary.gov/eisenhowers/quotes.

3 Theodore Roosevelt Center, "Man in the Arena," https://www
.theodorerooseveltcenter.org/Learn-About-TR/TR-Encyclopedia
/Culture-and-Society/Man-in-the-Arena.aspx.

CHAPTER 3: BREAKERS AND BUILDERS

1 Mike LaChance, "Useless Former Speaker Paul Ryan Bashes Trump
as 'Authoritarian' and Praises Rinos Adam Kinzinger and Liz Cheney,"
Gateway Pundit, December 14, 2023. https://www.thegatewaypundit
.com/2023/12/useless-former-speaker-paul-ryan-bashes-trump-as.

2 "Here's Donald Trump's Presidential Announcement Speech," *Time*,
June 16, 2015, https://time.com/3923128/donald-trump-announcement
-speech.

3 "'Less COVID, More Hunting': South Dakota Governor Gives Her
Take on Social Distancing," *USA Today*, October 6, 2020, https://
www.usatoday.com/videos/news/politics/2020/10/06/less-covid-more
-hunting-south-dakota-governor-gives-her-take-social-distancing
/3514284001.

4 Theodore Roosevelt, "Citizenship in a Republic" (speech), Sorbonne,
Paris, April 23, 1910, https://www.presidency.ucsb.edu/documents
/address-the-sorbonne-paris-france-citizenship-republic.

CHAPTER 4: GAS STATIONS, GUN SHOPS, AND GOVERNORS

1 Annie Todd, "Fact Check: Did South Dakota Governor Candidate
Jamie Smith Actually Say He Wanted to Raise Taxes?" *Argus Leader*,
October 21, 2022, https://www.argusleader.com/story/news/politics
/2022/10/21/south-dakota-governor-kristi-noem-ad-attacks-jamie-smith
-stating-wanted-to-raise-taxes-election-2022/69577223007.

2 "The Wise Words of Ronald Reagan," *Washington Times*, October 29,
2021, https://www.washingtontimes.com/news/2021/oct/29/wise-words
-ronald-reagan.

3 Laurel Thatcher Ulrich, "Vertuous Women Found: New England
Ministerial Literature, 1668–1735," *American Quarterly* 28, no. 1 (1976):
20–40, https://doi.org/10.2307/2712475.

4 Bureau of Labor Statistics, "Local Area Unemployment Statistics,"
January 23, 2024, https://www.bls.gov/web/laus/laumstrk.htm. https://
www.bls.gov/web/laus/laumstrk.htm; "South Dakota's Economy
Continues to Thrive," South Dakota State News, https://news.sd.gov
/news?id=news_kb_article_view&sysparm_article=KB0040555.

5 South Dakota Department of Labor and Regulation, "South Dakota Highlights of BLS Survey on Business Response to the Coronavirus Pandemic," December 7, 2020, https://dlr.sd.gov/lmic/sd_highlights_bls _survey.aspx.

6 US Bureau of Economic Analysis, "Personal Income by State," December 22, 2023, https://www.bea.gov/data/income-saving/personal -income-by-state.

7 "Governor Noem Grateful for President Trump's Continued Leadership on COVID-19 Recovery," South Dakota State News, August 14, 2020, https://news.sd.gov/news?id=news_kb_article_view& sys_id=6095a54c1bdc69506e4aa97ae54bcbed.

8 Alix Martichoux and Addy Bink, "35,000 People Moved to South Dakota Last Year. Where Did They Come From?" KELOLAND News, Oct 27, 2023, https://www.keloland.com/news/local-news/35000 -people-moved-to-south-dakota-last-year-where-did-they-come-from.

9 US House of Representatives, "H.R.6528 - PRC Accountability and Divestment Act of 2023," https://www.congress.gov/bill/118th-congress /house-bill/6528; "Gov. Noem Endorses Rep. Dusty Johnson's Bill to Block State Investments in Communist China," South Dakota State News, November 30, 2023, https://news.sd.gov/news?id=news_kb _article_view&sys_id=f260ce421b7afd104ebeecace54bcb3e.

10 "South Dakota Attorney General Removed from Office over Fatal Crash," *Politico*, June 21, 2022, https://www.politico.com/news/2022 /06/21/south-dakota-attorney-general-impeached-00041243; Joe Sneve, "What We Know about the Year-Long Saga surrounding AG Jason Ravnsborg's Role in Fatal Crash," *Argus Leader*, September 3, 2021, https://www.argusleader.com/story/news/2021/09/03/south-dakota -attorney-general-jason-ravnsborg-accident-tickets-kristi-noem-joseph -boever/5700492001.

CHAPTER 5: COVID AS A CASE STUDY

1 Gretchen Whitmer (@GovWhitmer), "This evening, I tested positive for COVID-19," Twitter, August 8, 2022, https://twitter.com /GovWhitmer/status/1556832198522699777.

2 Cory Meyers and Annie Todd, "South Dakota's History with 'Saturday Night Live.' It's Not Just Gov. Kristi Noem Impersonation," *Argus Leader*, October 3, 2022, https://www.argusleader.com/story /news/politics/2022/10/03/snl-impersonated-south-dakota-governor -kristi-noem-saturday-night-live/69535235007.

3 "'This Week' Transcript 11-8-20: Gov. Andrew Cuomo, Sen. Chris Coons, Gov. Kristi Noem, and Sen. Roy Blunt," ABC News, November 8, 2020, https://abcnews.go.com/Politics/week-transcript-11-20-gov -andrew-cuomo-sen/story?id=74089407.

4 Ryan A. Decker and John Haltiwanger, "Business Entry and Exit in the COVID-19 Pandemic: A Preliminary Look at Official Data," Federal Reserve, May 06, 2022, https://www.federalreserve.gov/econres /notes/feds-notes/business-entry-and-exit-in-the-covid-19-pandemic -a-preliminary-look-at-official-data-20220506.html.

5 Brett Samuels, "Trump Knocks Fauci: 'I Inherited Him,'" *The Hill*, August 31, 2020, https://thehill.com/homenews/administration/514523 -trump-knocks-fauci-i-inherited-him.

6 Joe Schoffstall, "Fauci and Wife's Net Worth Increased by $5M during the Pandemic, Analysis Finds," Fox News, September 29, 2022, https://www.foxnews.com/politics/fauci-wifes-net-worth-increased-5m -pandemic-analysis-finds.

7 Craig Chapple, "TikTok Crosses 2 Billion Downloads after Best Quarter for Any App Ever," Sensor Tower Blog, April 30, 2020, https:// sensortower.com/blog/tiktok-downloads-2-billion.

CHAPTER 6: WILL THE WORLD AWAKEN?

1 Barack Obama, "President Barack Obama's Inaugural Address," January 20, 2009, National Archives, https://obamawhitehouse.archives .gov/blog/2009/01/21/president-Barack-obamas-inaugural-address.

2 Tim Hains, "Argentine President-Elect Milei: 'I Didn't Come Here to Guide Lambs, but to Awaken Lions,'" RealClearPolitics, November 24, 2023, https://www.realclearpolitics.com/video/2023/11/24/argentine _president-elect_milei_i_didnt_come_here_to_guide_lambs_but_to _awaken_lions.html.

3 Jacob Newton, "Gov. Kristi Noem Headlines Right-Wing Summit in France," KELOLAND News, November 10, 2023, https://www .keloland.com/keloland-com-original/gov-kristi-noem-headlines-right -wing-summit-in-france.

4 Oren Liebermann, "Only 43 of more than 8,000 Discharged from US Military for Refusing Covid Vaccine Have Rejoined," CNN, October 2, 2023, https://www.cnn.com/2023/10/02/politics/us-military-covid -vaccine/index.html.

5 The Land Report, "Tianqiao Chen," Land Report, 2021, https:// landreport.com/land-report-100/tianqiao-chen.

6 Peter Aitken, "Biden Stresses US 'Does Not Support Independence' for Taiwan as World Leaders React to Election Win," Fox News, January 13, 2024, https://www.foxnews.com/world/biden-stresses-us -does-not-support-independence-taiwan-world-leaders-react-election -win.

7 Chloe Mayer, "Ted Cruz Hails 'Spectacular' Giorgia Meloni as GOP Finds Potential Ally," *Newsweek*, September 26, 2022, https://www .newsweek.com/ted-cruz-giogia-meloni-spectacular-1746162.

8 James Carafano and Stefano Graziosi, "Italy's Prime Minister Wisely Spurns Deal with China," *Daily Signal*, December 28, 2023, https:// www.dailysignal.com/2023/12/28/italys-prime-minister-wisely-spurns -deal-with-china/.

CHAPTER 7: THE WOLF PACK

1 Abby Phillip, "Internet Takes Off with Mitt Romney's 'Binders Full of Women,'" ABC News, October 17, 2012, https://abcnews.go.com/blogs /politics/2012/10/internet-takes-off-with-mitt-romneys-binders-full-of -women.

2 Supreme Court of the United States, "Sandra Day O'Connor: First Woman on the Supreme Court," https://www.supremecourt.gov /visiting/exhibitions/SOCExhibit/Section4.aspx.

3 Abby Wambach, *Wolfpack: How to Come Together, Unleash Our Power, and Change the Game* (New York: Celadon Books, 2019).

4 Tim Alberta, "Nikki Haley's Time for Choosing," *Politico*, February 2021, https://www.politico.com/interactives/2021/magazine-nikki -haleys-choice.

5 John McCormick, "Nikki Haley Embraces Trump in Her Vision of GOP Future," *Wall Street Journal*, October 5, 2021, https://www.wsj .com/articles/nikki-haley-embraces-trump-in-her-vision-of-gop-future -11633424400.

6 Brie Stimson, "Nikki Haley Raises Eyebrows with 'Change Personalities' Comment as Her Momentum Sparks Increased Scrutiny," Fox News, January 6, 2024, https://www.foxnews.com /politics/nikki-haley-raises-eyebrows-change-personalities-comment -momentum-sparks-increased-scrutiny.

7 Margaret Thatcher, "Margaret Thatcher, in Her Own Words," *Washington Post*, April 8, 2013, https://www.washingtonpost.com /national/on-leadership/margaret-thatchers-best-quotes/2013/04/08 /97abce78-a07d-11e2-82bc-511538ae90a4_story.html.

8 Women's Congressional Policy Institute, "Women, Peace, and Security Act Clears Senate," August 3, 2017, https://www.wcpinst.org/source /women-peace-security-act-clears-senate; "Schakowsky, Noem Lead House in Passing the Women, Peace, and Security Act" (press release), Congresswoman Jan Schakowsky (website), November 15, 2016, https:// schakowsky.house.gov/media/press-releases/schakowsky-noem-lead -house-passing-women-peace-and-security-act.

CHAPTER 8: JUST BECAUSE YOU'RE PARANOID

1 Jeffrey Clark, "Nancy Pelosi Instructs Americans to Vote on How Politics Will Impact 'Your Life,' Not 'Your Religion,'" Fox News, March 29, 2023, https://www.foxnews.com/media/nancy-pelosi -instructs-americans-vote-how-politics-impact-your-life-not-your -religion.

2 "Interview for *Woman's Own*," September 23, 1987, Margaret Thatcher Foundation, https://www.margaretthatcher.org/document/106689.

3 Joseph Heller, *Catch-22* (New York: Simon & Schuster, 2011).

4 "Interview for *Woman's Own*," September 23, 1987, Margaret Thatcher Foundation, https://www.margaretthatcher.org/document/106689.

CHAPTER 9: DONKEYS, RINOS, AND BISON

1 "CNN Covers the Fourth Republican Presidential Debate" (transcript), CNN, December 6, 2023, https://transcripts.cnn.com/show /se/date/2023-12-06/segment/02.

2 Eric Garcia, "Mitt Romney Says Endorsement in 2024 GOP Primary Would Be 'Kiss of Death,'" *The Independent*, December 14, 2023, https://www.the-independent.com/news/world/americas/us-politics/mitt -romney-gop-primary-endorsement-b2464348.html.

3 "10 Famous People Who Switched Political Parties," National Constitution Center, March 20, 2015, https://constitutioncenter.org /blog/10-famous-people-who-switch-political-parties.

4 "Oregon Mom Appeals to 9th Circuit: End Ideological Litmus Test, Let Children Find Forever Homes" (press release), Alliance Defending Freedom, December 13, 2023, https://adflegal.org/press-release/oregon -mom-appeals-9th-circuit-end-ideological-litmus-test-let-children-find -forever.

5 Katelynn Richardson, "'War on Families': Federal 'Home Visiting' Program Classifies Parents Who Don't Let Young Kids Cross-Dress as Potentially Abusive," *Daily Caller*, December 20, 2023, https://

dailycaller.com/2023/12/20/federal-home-visiting-program-classifies
-parents-young-kids-cross-dress-potentially-abusive.

6 Hannah Grossman, "Female Recruit Considered Resigning after
Being Forced to Shower with Trans Women with Full Male Genitalia,"
Fox News, July 17, 2023, https://www.foxnews.com/media/female
-recruit-considered-resigning-being-forced-shower-trans-women-full
-male-genitalia.

7 Clyde Wayne Crews, "Ten Thousand Commandments 2023,"
Competitive Enterprise Institute, October 29, 2023, https://cei.org
/studies/ten-thousand-commandments-2023.

8 Will Doran, "Biden Won't Face Any Competition in NC's 2024
Democratic Primary, State Election Officials Confirm," WRAL,
January 2, 2024, https://www.wral.com/story/biden-won-t-face-any
-competition-in-nc-s-2024-democratic-primary-state-election-officials
-confirm/21218264.

9 Lauren Camera, "Garland Defends Decision to Mobilize FBI against
Threats to School Board Members," *US News and World Report*,
October 21, 2021, https://www.usnews.com/news/education-news
/articles/2021-10-21/garland-defends-decision-to-mobilize-fbi-against
-threats-to-school-board-members.

10 Steve Karnowski, "Minnesota Governor Criticizes South Dakota
Counterpart," Associated Press, November 11, 2020, https://apnews
.com/article/virus-outbreak-st-paul-south-dakota-minnesota-kristi
-noem-b227daf6139be0d6ccce2e80800356ae.

11 Mike LaChance, "Useless Former Speaker Paul Ryan Bashes
Trump as 'Authoritarian' and Praises Rinos Adam Kinzinger and
Liz Cheney," Gateway Pundit, December 14, 2023, https://www
.thegatewaypundit.com/2023/12/useless-former-speaker-paul-ryan
-bashes-trump-as.

12 George Washington, "Farewell Address," September 17, 1796, Mount
Vernon, Virginia, https://www.senate.gov/artandhistory/history
/resources/pdf/Washingtons_Farewell_Address.pdf.

13 *New State Ice Co. v. Liebmann*, 285 US 262, 311 (1932), https://supreme
.justia.com/cases/federal/us/285/262.

14 Jeffrey Jones, "U.S. Political Party Preferences Shifted Greatly during
2021," Gallup, January 17, 2022, https://news.gallup.com/poll/388781
/political-party-preferences-shifted-greatly-during-2021.aspx.

15 Elon Musk (@elonmusk), "In the USA, you don't need government
issued ID to vote and you can mail in your ballot. This is

insane," X, January 8, 2024, https://twitter.com/elonmusk/status
/1744498282141786473.

16 Stephen Groves, "Noem Signs Bill Banning Election Donations Like
Zuckerberg's," AP News, March 16, 2022, https://apnews.com/article
/2022-midterm-elections-covid-technology-health-media-de9b51cda0e
a0e88782e4bd052a0ba09.

CHAPTER 10: FREEDOM OF SPEECH AND EDUCATION

1 Joshua Q. Nelson, "Teachers Union Boss Randi Weingarten Claims
School Choice 'Undermines Democracy,'" Fox News, December 19,
2023, https://www.foxnews.com/media/teacher-union-boss-randi
-weingarten-claims-school-choice-undermines-democracy.

2 Bill Clinton, "State of the Union Address," January 23, 1996, National
Archives, https://clintonwhitehouse4.archives.gov/WH/New/other/sotu
.html.

3 Mike Lee, "Achieving Choice in Education Act (ACE Act)," December
2023, https://www.lee.senate.gov/services/files/41E9C5E9-4CD6-4873
-8481-92FDCB7C91B8; "A Bill to Amend the Internal Revenue Code of
1986 to Provide Incentives for Education," https://www.lee.senate.gov
/services/files/A4F89A2D-F2CF-418C-9799-10662292D861.

4 Josh Christenson, "Nearly 6,000 US Public Schools Hide Child's
Gender Status from Parents," *New York Post*, March 8, 2023, https://
nypost.com/2023/03/08/us-public-schools-conceal-childs-gender-status
-from-parents.

5 Joshua Q. Nelson, "Pennsylvania School Board President Sworn into
Office with Sexually Explicit Book," Fox News, December 6, 2023,
https://www.foxnews.com/media/pennsylvania-school-board-president
-sworn-into-office-sexually-explicit-book.

6 Dana Perino, *Everything Will Be Okay: Life Lessons for Young Women
(from a Former Young Woman)* (Grand Central, 2021).

CHAPTER 11: THE MOST POWERFUL PERSON IN GOVERNMENT

1 Josh Cohen, "'So Angry': Chris Matthews Says Dealing with Rural
Americans Is Like 'Fighting Terrorism,'" *Daily Caller*, December 26,
2023, https://dailycaller.com/2023/12/26/chris-matthews-dealing-rural
-americans-fighting-terrorism.

2 Tucker Carlson (@TuckerCarlson), "A government that cares about
you tries to elevate you. [. . .] Anyone who's trying to make you

dependent is trying to hurt you," X, December 19, 2023, https://twitter
.com/TuckerCarlson/status/1737070890196582670.

3 John F. Kennedy, "President John F. Kennedy's Inaugural Address
(1961)," January 20, 1961, National Archives, https://www.archives.gov
/milestone-documents/president-john-f-kennedys-inaugural-address.

4 Stephen R. Covey, *The 7 Habits of Highly Effective People* (Free Press,
1989).

5 Mallory Simon, "Over 1,000 Health Professionals Sign a Letter
Saying, Don't Shut Down Protests Using Coronavirus Concerns as an
Excuse," CNN, June 5, 2020, https://www.cnn.com/2020/06/05/health
/health-care-open-letter-protests-coronavirus-trnd/index.html.

CHAPTER 12: LEADING FORWARD

1 Charles Hilu, "Biden Tells Voters 'I Work for the Government in the
Senate,'" *Washington Free Beacon*, January 12, 2024, https://freebeacon
.com/latest-news/watch-biden-tells-voters-i-work-for-the-government
-in-the-senate.

CHAPTER 13: INTO THE FRAY

1 Joe Carnahan, director, *The Grey*, 2011.

2 "Margaret Thatcher (1925–2013)," Margaret Thatcher Foundation,
https://www.margaretthatcher.org/archive/MTobit.

3 Robert Coram, *Boyd: The Fighter Pilot Who Changed the Art of War*
(Boston: Back Bay Books, 2004).

CHAPTER 14: DAY ONE

1 Eric Bradner, "Biden: Lindsey Graham Will 'Regret His Whole Life'
Doing Trump's Bidding on Ukraine," CNN, November 23, 2019,
https://www.cnn.com/2019/11/22/politics/joe-biden-don-lemon-cnntv
/index.html.

2 Jill Colvin and Bill Barrow, "Trump's Vow to Only Be a Dictator on
'Day One' Follows Growing Worry over His Authoritarian Rhetoric,"
Associated Press, December 7, 2023, https://apnews.com/article/trump
-hannity-dictator-authoritarian-presidential-election-f27e7e9d7c13fabb
e3ae7dd7f1235c72.

3 Miriam Valverde, "Here's What Donald Trump Did in his First Week
as President of the United States," Politifact, January 27, 2017, https://
www.politifact.com/article/2017/jan/27/heres-what-donald-trump-did
-first-week-president-u.

4 The White House, "Fact Sheet: President-Elect Biden's Day One Executive Actions," White House, January 20, 2021, https://www .whitehouse.gov/briefing-room/statements-releases/2021/01/20/fact -sheet-president-elect-bidens-day-one-executive-actions-deliver-relief -for-families-across-america-amid-converging-crises.

APPENDIX B

1 Press Release, "Governor Kristi Noem Announces New Education Plan," South Dakota Department of Education, January 9, 2024, https://news.sd.gov/news?id=news_kb_article_view&sys_id=93b5584b1 b2fb51031b1ebdbac4bcb8c.

ACKNOWLEDGMENTS

There are so many people who support and inspire me on a daily basis, I simply can't list you all here. If you've turned to this page and your name isn't here, I'm sorry to disappoint. I love you all dearly, and hope you know that.

There are also others who never expect thanks. They not only text, call, and check in—they show up, inconvenience themselves, and let me be their friend. They also encourage me and tell me I'm doing great when it feels like I'm failing (bunch of fibbers!). It's a rare thing these days to have people in your life you can really trust. I am a blessed woman.

These ladies understand that I need them to help me stay strong—and that it's okay to be a girl. In fact it's pretty awesome. Brittany, Jodi, Melissa, Beth, Linda, Leslie, and McKenzye. You all are superheroes. Keep using your powers for good.

Oh, I should also thank the folks who helped me write this book!

I didn't know writing a book could be fun! First of all, the best agent ever, Tom Winters, introduced me to Alex Pappas and the Hachette team, who convinced me I had something interesting to say. Then they presented a timeline that no one thought was achievable. *Challenge accepted!*

Tom introduced me to a crazy guy named Mike Loomis, who agreed to help, and the rest is history. Mike's ability to tolerate my schedule is profound, and he even scolded me once for not being prepared on having material written! I determined after that to never let him down again. He made this process enjoyable. (When is our next project starting?)

And shout out to Ian: thanks for keeping me honest!

Finally, to you, my reader friend. Thank you for turning these pages with me. I look forward to hearing about the bold steps you're taking to move forward.

ABOUT THE AUTHOR

GOVERNOR KRISTI NOEM is a rancher, farmer, small business owner, wife, mom, grandma, and *New York Times* bestselling author of *Not My First Rodeo: Lessons from the Heartland.*

In 2010, after serving in the South Dakota legislature for several years, Noem was elected to serve as South Dakota's lone member of the US House of Representatives. During her time in Congress, in addition to many other successes, Governor Noem helped pass the Tax Cuts and Jobs Act, which put $2,400 back in the pockets of the average South Dakota family.

In 2018, with the platform of protecting South Dakotans against tax increases, government growth, federal intrusion, and government secrecy, she was elected as South Dakota's first-ever female governor.

In 2022, Governor Noem was reelected with the largest vote total in the history of South Dakota. Each new office brought an ever-evolving set of responsibilities, but the mission has remained constant: make South Dakota a better place. Every policy decision and executive strategy is undertaken with that end goal in mind.

As governor, Noem has honored the rights of her people by trusting them to exercise their personal responsibility to make the best decisions for themselves, their loved ones, and—in turn—their communities. She has focused on building stronger families, better education, and keeping South Dakota "Open for Business."

Governor Noem fought against federal tax increases, and she is fiercely protective of preserving a system of no state income tax. She's a staunch supporter of the Second Amendment and is steadfast in maintaining constitutional carry rights. She's unwavering in her commitment to personal freedom and will always fight against government intrusion.

Under Governor Noem's leadership, South Dakota has served as a great example to the nation of what can be accomplished when you follow the governing philosophies our founders set in place. God bestows individual liberty, and people should be able to exercise their freedoms without bureaucratic interference. Government's role is to serve the people, working for them to provide opportunities for a better future.

The prosperity of South Dakota and our nation is important to her for the same reason it's important to every American: it's home.

Despite all of this, Governor Noem often says that her greatest accomplishment is raising her three children, Kassidy, Kennedy, and Booker, with her husband, Bryon. All have a deep love for their family and an even deeper love for the Lord.

KristiNoem.com

FreedomWorksHere.com